Lessons My Brothers Taught Me

LESSONS
MY BROTHERS
TAUGHT ME

How to Transform Your
Personal Qualities Into A
Successful Business

CHARLES D. McCARRICK

HOUNDSTOOTH
PRESS

Hardcover ISBN: 978-1-5445-3339-1
Paperback ISBN: 978-1-5445-3340-7
Ebook ISBN: 978-1-5445-3341-4

Illustrations by C. Henning McCarrick

To Mary Ann

Contents

FOREWORD

by Dick McCarrick

BACK IN OUR GARAGE BAND DAYS, MY BROTHER CHARLIE used to say that everyone has at least one good song in them. Today I'd amend that to add that they also have at least one good story to tell. And by "good" I mean one that's interesting, insightful, and entertaining.

This book is Charlie's story, and I think it meets all three of those criteria. The basic narrative is certainly interesting since it's a latter-day example of the classic rags-to-riches tale: a kid from an impoverished New England backwater grows up in what at best would be described as lower middle-class circumstances; an indifferent student who drops out of college after a handful of classes is, by his mid-twenties, seemingly well on his way to life as a blue-collar everyman. Then suddenly he presses the reset button and goes back to college at an age where most of us have left schooling far in the rear-view mirror. Upon graduation he lands a dream job and within a few years is considered a world expert in his technical field. Eventually he starts his own company and navigates it through a variety of trials and errors to an eight-figure net worth. What's not to love?

Of course, the basic sequence of events is only part of the reason we're interested in stuff like this. We also want to know *how* it happened. Or, more to the point, *what can I learn from this that will help me achieve my own goals and dreams?* This is where books of this type typically falter. Many of them present events so extraordinary they have no relevance to everyday experience; they may as well be describing hobbits and unicorns. Others fail in the other direction, providing bland banalities akin to "work hard and eat your vegetables." Clearly, it isn't easy for successful people to explain their success in a way the rest of us can understand.

I can personally sympathize. I had a front-row seat to most of the events described in this book, often playing Mycroft Holmes to Charlie's Sherlock. Yet before reading this book, I'd be hard-pressed to even begin to explain how he did it. About the best I could offer would be to say that, like a lot of highly successful and creative people, Charlie is an excellent joiner of ideas, able to take things learned in one part of his life and apply them to completely unrelated areas. Here's an example. One time, Charlie was struggling with an antenna design under an impending deadline. The holdup was this one component, which had a very particular set of specifications for size, shape, weight, flexibility, and so on. As he considered the problem, it occurred to him that these specs reminded him of a device with which he was very familiar in a very different application. You see, Charlie happens to be an avid angler, and the specs pretty much described a fishing pole. A quick trip to the tackle shop procured some fishing pole blanks. They worked perfectly! Project saved, customer happy.

Charlie has infused that same philosophy into this book. Throughout, he explains how he has applied lessons learned throughout his life—including some that form his earliest childhood memories—to solve seemingly unrelated business problems. This theme makes this book especially valuable and accessible to us common folk. We may not have experienced the exact same set of life events Charlie describes, but each of us has similarly learned things at various stages of our lives that left lasting impressions. *Thus, every one of us already has the knowledge to help us succeed in business if we simply know when and how to use it.* This is a radical, even subversive, idea since it suggests that, irrespective of your business training or education, you can still be successful if you know how to take advantage of the things you've already learned elsewhere. That's not to imply that business training is worthless, of course. Had Charlie possessed an MBA, he might have been able to foresee and avoid some of the issues that threatened to derail his business. Then again, it's quite possible that he'd also have talked himself out of taking some of the more audacious steps critical to his eventual success.

It's a point that bears repeating: each of us already possesses the pieces from which we can build our own success. Out of context that probably sounds like some New Age "The Secret"-type claptrap. But within a few minutes of starting this book, you'll soon see that is very much not what it's about. You'll also learn a couple of other things about Charlie. One, he's extremely intelligent. And two, he has zero pretensions. On one page you'll find a thoughtful, detailed discussion of how to make a critical business decision. On another, you'll learn what it's like to have dog feces fly into your mouth (although don't expect Charlie to use polite words like "feces" when more colorful vocabulary is readily available). Yet somehow it all ties together and makes perfect sense. Few books cover such a broad spectrum of topics while always keeping a central theme in full focus. And for readers with the right frame of mind, it just may be your guide for achieving your goals in business—or any other field in which your definition of success may lie.

—Dick McCarrick
March 2020

INTRODUCTION

MY BROTHERS WERE PASSIONATE ABOUT MY EDUCATION. They never tired of devising novel lessons for me, many concluding in an obligatory torment essential to driving home some critical point. There is nothing special or unusual about this, as every younger sibling knows. It's a time-honored tradition spanning countless generations, tracing all the way back to Cain and Abel. I was a slow learner, apparently, and it took many years before I could appreciate the lesson part as opposed to focusing exclusively on the torment. As often as not, I received what was coming to me and must confess to instigating my own share of the hijinks. I could hardly be described as an innocent bystander in these events; a more accurate description would be an unidentified suspect attempting to blend in with the crowd of curious onlookers at a crime scene. In time, the principles beneath these experiences would become clear and serve me well by providing guidance through the most difficult business decisions I would face.

Thought-provoking books tend to be those that present subject matter in a narrative interspersed with quips, quotes, and anecdotes to keep things interesting and alive. This book is sort of the opposite. It is a string of anecdotes imbued with occasional bits of subject matter, woven into a story. It is an attempt toward putting into words the remarkable evolution of my career from unemployed to Captain of Industry. Okay, maybe Captain is a stretch, but certainly a seat close to the Captain's table. What makes my story noteworthy is that, despite lacking any sense for business or formal training in that field, I played an essential role in building a company from nothing more than an idea into an eight-figure high-tech enterprise. This by itself is hardly a credential for writing a book about business (or much else, for that matter). There must be dozens of books in circulation by individuals who, through a combination of skill and circumstance, created a successful company and then had the urge to write about it. However, what worked for these authors is unlikely to work for most readers, as the set of circumstances leading to their success is unique to their story and difficult to translate into yours.

So how is this book different from those? Well, maybe it's not, but at the very least the reader should find it entertaining and might even learn something from the blunders I made and how they were corrected. The mistakes I made early on were abundant and taught me much. They taught me to stick with what I know and partner with people who are intelligent, trustworthy, and capable of helping with those aspects of the business in which I am less skilled.

This is a story about building Micro-Ant, a company I founded, from nothing more than a dream and the sheer will to succeed. It's also a story about making terrible mistakes and recovering from them. Most of all it describes how all success is built upon the foundation of basic principles and sustained by the character of individuals participating in a common goal. It is written for the retired Coast Guard Captain looking to start a fishing charter business or the young bank teller spending his days off creating a line of bow ties or the enterprising caretaker trying to launch a full-service landscaping business. In other words, anyone who is determined to form and run their own business despite lacking any previous experience pertinent to doing so.

Many people have asked for my advice on how to *start* a business. Oddly, I am rarely asked how to *succeed* in business. There is a difference, but I generally assume the latter is what people really want to know so I frame my answer in that context. The budding entrepreneur should first ask themselves, "*Why* do I want to go into business?" People generally do it because they feel restricted in some way by their current situation, perhaps earning potential, creative expression, work environment, or simply the freedom to make decisions that govern their professional and personal well-being. Knowing what you want to achieve personally should stipulate your plan on how to proceed professionally.

* * *

LIFE LESSON: We grew up in a rural area that was deforested here and there to make space for farming and human habitation. About two acres surrounding our house had been cleared to provide areas for gardening, fruit trees, and other sundries for sustaining an existence in the middle of nowhere. My older brothers, Hank and Bill, transformed a large portion of this outdoor space into an all-inclusive Olympic arena, with high jump, broad jump, pole vault, discus, shot put, javelin throwing, and an oval track for hundred-yard dashes. It was Team Hank against Team Bill, with Hank matched against Bill and Dick against me in the various events. I was three years junior to my brother Dick, so he would best me in all events except running. I would invariably edge him out in every heat despite Hank encouraging Dick's progress from behind with a holly branch. *(I had my share of these encouragements as well.)* We weren't competing to win; we were competing not to lose. Losing meant being awarded the Golden Medal of Defeat, which meant the victors would urinate on a stick that the vanquished had to pick up with their teeth and hold there while the winning team mouth-trumpeted the Olympic theme song. Such was the temperament of most contests between us boys, so the wiser course of action was to vanish whenever my older brothers were in a gaming mood. Any activity Dick or I might be engaged in, no matter how innocuous, would immediately be transformed into a contest if observed by Bill or Hank. By "contest" I mean "torment," which was the true objective in their enhancement of our activities. Let me illustrate the point: Dick and I set up a putting range in our front yard. The goal was to get your ball into the coffee can taking the fewest strokes. Bill saw our game and joined in uninvited, commandeering my putter and ball. He was leading Dick by a stroke and lined up for the final putt but missed. Dick made a noise which to me sounded like a sneeze, but Bill construed it as a snort. In declaration of Dick's victory, Bill picked up the golf ball and, within easy putting range, threw it into Dick's eye socket, simultaneously delivering a hole-in-one and a black eye. Interestingly, Dick and I averaged four strokes per round but against Bill, Dick was at six strokes. He was attempting to throw the game in Bill's favor because he knew that winning meant losing. As it turned out, losing meant losing too, and if there was a winner at all in this instance, it was me, who bolted off like a scalded dog at the sight of Bill stooping for the golf ball.

MORAL: Playing not to lose is different than playing to win. Similarly, a strategy based on not failing is different than a strategy based on succeeding. Your determination to succeed must form the basis of your plan.

* * *

BEFORE EMBARKING ON ANYTHING NEAR as monumental as starting your own business, you should first begin with a self-assessment of what personal qualities exist in your toolbox that can be employed to your benefit. These qualities, character traits, attributes, or however you wish to label them are the most valuable assets at your disposal applicable toward succeeding at, well, just about anything. The following chapters describe my journey of discovering and employing the traits that make me who I am and upon which my entrepreneurial success is built. You must go through a similar exercise to discover your own special set of tools, and I will explain how to transform these into a strategy for succeeding in your business venture. Let's begin by understanding what a business is and isn't, and how the elements of its success rely greatly on how you conduct yourself as an individual.

An online search of the principles necessary for building a successful business will result in lists of items numbering anywhere from six to twenty-one. Although most of these are common sense and do impart good advice, there still needs to be a strategy for compiling them into a coherent plan that works and is easy to follow. To develop your own personalized plan, you must be able to relate these principles to your own strengths in order to determine those where you excel and those where you are deficient. Applying principles effectively toward establishing a profitable and culturally successful business depends largely on how we apply our human attributes. These are the traits or qualities we each develop throughout life, whether or not older siblings are involved. Of the many principles described in the literature for launching and running a business, I propose boiling it down to the following four:

- *Salability*

- *Sensibility*

- *Sustainability*

- *Scalability*

Let's call them the *4Ss*, which is a nice hook and easy to remember since they conveniently all start with the letter "S."

Although bullet-listed here in a linear sequence, they are better comprehended as components in a circulatory flow process we'll call the *4S Transform*, as shown in the diagram below. Within the transform operation, each principle is an operative building upon the one preceding it, developing greater potential with each step much like the *flywheel effect* described in Jim Collins's number one bestseller, *Good to Great*. The transform is a process or roadmap connecting two seemingly independent domains, beginning at an origin and leading to a destination. In the framework presented here, the originating domain is comprised of human qualities such as the personal traits exemplified by you and your team while the destination domain is comprised of qualities that characterize your company. The 4Ss then are components of a four-part process that together provide a path that transforms between personal input and professional outcome. This might smack of the New Age claptrap Dick warned us about in his Foreword, but you have likely abided by these principles or something similar for much of your private life. In any case, I'll try to keep this dense but important concept brief.

In diagram form, the 4S Transform looks like this:

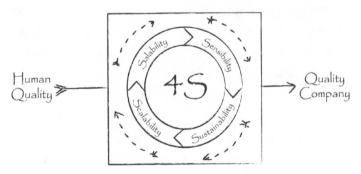

The 4S Transform is a tool meant to convert your personal qualities into a successful business.

1. Salability

The first principle is having a valued product, one that has *salability*. That product is *you*. You must "market" yourself to be viewed as a valued asset and not a mere obstacle or, worse, a liability, in which case the only "business" transacted will be wholly undesirable. It means having a positive attitude and being dependable, supporting whatever occurrence or opportunity might arise and participating toward an outcome that benefits all parties. Will this guarantee smooth business transactions and spare you from torment? Hell no! But it can go a long way toward developing far more favorable relationships and terms. Developing good character in youth pays enormous dividends in adulthood and is essential for any good leader or entrepreneur to succeed. Bear in mind it is never too late to develop these good traits, as the dividing age between youth and adulthood is somewhat gray. I did not make the transition myself until thirty.

No matter what services or goods your company might sell, *you* are in the final product. Included in every sale as an added value is a piece of who you are and what you and your business stand for. Reliability, integrity, and pride should shine through in everything you deliver, no matter the market or the product, and are often key differentiators over your competition. Offering consistent, reliable service should be a given, and your customers should come to expect this if you want to win and keep their business. But do not forget integrity! When something goes wrong due to a mishap (big or small), make that an opportunity to really shine by demonstrating that you do not walk away and leave the customer hanging, that you are committed to their satisfaction, and that you will not give up until that commitment is met. How a company responds when things go bad says a lot more about its character than how its employees conduct themselves when everything is rosy and delightful. Anyone who has had to spend minutes or even hours waiting to speak to a nameless, faceless customer service agent knows exactly what I'm talking about. As often as not the agent you finally get a hold of has no control over your issue and therefore is inadequately equipped to solve your problem. Don't do this to your customers. Show them that you are better than this, that you care about them as people and recognize that their time is valuable and their patronage is appreciated.

2. Sensibility

Another important principle is having *sensibility* with regard to your industry through knowing your customers, respecting your competitors, and being sensible of how you fit into it all. For instance, entering a game of golf with Bill was an unwise venture on all counts, whereas a round or two with Dick generally had a far more profitable return. Bill was a difficult customer to deal with, but under more favorable terms, could have had much to offer. The only certainty in a transaction with Bill was that you lost. The key is to tailor each transaction according to the parties involved so that everybody wins.

Many companies believe that a successful deal is one in which the other party loses something. A zero-sum game. They do not foster relationships; they fester them. A small business just starting out that, like the youngest sibling, tends to end up with the burning end of the firestick, needs to be especially wary of these characters. Structuring a good deal has less to do with company size than it does quality of character because the success of any business transaction is ultimately based upon the integrity and intellectual wherewithal of the individuals making it, not the name or brand of the companies behind them. In the early stages of getting Micro-Ant off the ground, we dealt with a customer possessing the same disposition as my brother Bill. Ironically, their VP of engineering was also named Bill, and he took great delight in changing requirements on us mid-project or cleverly sneaking in contract terms meant to penalize us on a whim. Plus three-month payment terms. We endured this painful relationship for several years until our new CEO entered the scene and was able to establish a bilateral agreement favorable to all parties. Of course, this prompted that company to stop doing business with us, which was fine as far as we were concerned—once we came to our senses.

Going forward we developed scorecards for potential customers based on criteria we set for the sort of companies we wanted to do business with. We favored those who believed in fostering a good relationship as opposed to *bullying* the supplier into submission. Avoiding them outright was the wisest course of action but not always realistic, so learning to deal with difficult customers was (and is) a requisite for enjoying a prosperous future. I have a very dear friend who is a retired (he would say *recovering*) attorney who told me that the first thing he learned in business law was to practice confidentiality, meaning do not tell the other party anything you don't want them to know so that you can lead them into acting in a way that serves your interests. We nonlawyers call this *deception*. Look, I could go on and on about big-league businesses who outright stole our intellectual property and went so far as to patent it. They do it because they can. There is nothing we small businesses can do to stop it once in motion, and they know it. All the more reason to keep a heightened sense of awareness with who and what you are dealing with. The 4S Transform also works in reverse, meaning that the foundation and reputation of any business can be traced back to the people behind it.

* * *

LIFE LESSON: In our household, Murphy's Law was a forgone conclusion. McCarrick's Law went more like this: "If something can go wrong, it already has. You just weren't paying attention." The following illustrates this principle. My mother had an electric frying pan with a neat design feature I am sure has long since been outlawed. The appliance was equipped with a detachable power cord consisting of a cable for connecting to an AC outlet, a thermostat dial for setting cook temperature, and an exposed four-inch-long electrified probe that plugged into the pan to engage its built-in heating element. (One of my brothers claimed that our father invented it, but I can provide no evidence to support this.) Best of all, the probe could be detached from the pan to provide a high-voltage, super-hot wood-burning instrument. I would take it out to the garage and burn artwork into wooden planks, always careful not to touch the live probe. During one creative session, I took a break and left the probe plugged in next to my work. I then returned a minute later to see Bill reaching for the thing, apparently not realizing it was plugged in. Of the many possible responses at my disposal, I did not exercise any that might prevent Bill from being thermo-electrocuted. Blended in his screams were accusations that I knew the thing was live, which was true, and that I let him pick it up so that he would get shocked, also true. But this was all Bill's fault. He knew the system we brothers had in place. Hell, he was one of the chief architects of these bylaws and, of anyone, should have realized that if something could go wrong, it already had. Thermo-electrocution was the price for not paying better attention. Bill stepped toward me. I braced for it, but he walked on past into the house, probably to fish a piece of ice from the freezer to quell the burn. That was the end of it. All in all, I came off pretty well—maybe even *ahead* since it was a rare transaction when Bill did not profit from someone else's loss. In some respects, I was more shocked than he was.

MORAL: He who made kittens put snakes in the grass. He also put them in corporate legal departments. Remember, *their* policies don't have to be *yours*. Do not agree to terms that are biased against you.

* * *

3. Sustainability

The third principle for a business to be successful is *sustainability*. Sustainability basically means to maintain an existence. Money in and of itself is not sufficient or necessarily essential toward launching a business that can be sustained. I say this having started Micro-Ant with little money, using the assets I already possessed at home and my own life's experiences to forge forward. In a startup business, the ambition of seeing your vision become a reality is the main thing, the *driving force*. Being committed to success and possessing a stubborn determination to succeed is *essential*. You can always borrow money, but determination must come from within. Determination can sustain you for a very, very long time. But if you and the business are one and the same, you're in a situation that is not sustainable. You must grow the company beyond yourself.

I run a side business making duffle bags. It's called Swordy Moon. These are some decent bags, constructed from fine marine-grade materials built to withstand harsh environments. The Yeti of duffle bags. I've delivered hundreds of them to date, personally manufacturing each one on my sewing machine. My business plan is simple: take orders, purchase the materials online, handcraft every bag according to each customer's color choices, then give it away for free. Sounds like a pretty shitty business, right? Not to me. I think it's a great success because it provides me exactly what I am seeking out of this enterprise: freedom to express myself creatively while providing a valued product that someone will use and keep forever. Swordy Moon has all the elements of any legitimate business, and the lack of a positive net cash flow is incidental and not entirely atypical. The point is we are each bound to define success differently and in accordance with our own personal aspirations. Your business plan should be developed upon *your* definition of success. It so happens that Swordy Moon is sustained financially by my other business, Micro-Ant, or else it could not so easily exist. At my current production rate, I can fund bag production for the next thousand years.

Swordy Moon is therefore *not* a sustainable business from an economic perspective, at least in its current state—though the groundwork has been laid to make it so. Even though it is a personal achievement, it is not commercially viable, simply because it is not making money. It passes the test of sustainability in every other way except one: what if I quit? A business cannot be sustained if it's a one-person show, in which case it's arguable whether this is a business at all or rather a glorified job. What does it matter? None if that is your goal, but my narrative is intended more for entrepreneurs looking to start and build a business that in time will create equity, income, and jobs.

4. Scalability

If you are looking to create a legitimate business, meaning one that is salable, sensible, sustainable, and grows in value over time, then you should also have *scalability*. (The concept of scalability as it pertains to business is described nicely in *The Entrepreneur Equation* by Carol Roth.) Scalability in simple business terms means to change a company in size without compromising the intrinsic value of its products. Let's make sure we're clear on this point. A well-conceived, scalable manufacturing operation should be able to increase its production output by *scaling up* resources, e.g., floor space, line workers, raw materials, and assembly equipment, or just as well scale down production via reduction of these resources. The critical takeaway is that in both scenarios quantity is affected, but not quality. The product remains exactly the same, in no way compromised in terms of quality metrics such as performance, reliability, and so on. There may be a cost benefit to scaling up, but the product delivered, whether it is a service or finished goods, is the same in every respect as the original. A company with an appropriate scalability plan will have a much greater chance of increasing sales revenue and stimulating growth. But what does a good scalability plan look like? For different types of businesses, it could mean different things, but the common denominator is a team of good people following a good plan.

I have developed a free online tool to help you create your own personalized 4S Assessment. To access this tool, go to my website, CharlesMcCarrick.com. Samples are provided to help get you started, along with a short instructional video. At first, focus only on salability and sensibility since these are personal-oriented traits, whereas sustainability and scalability are oriented toward the business. You will deal with these two traits at a later time as your business vision begins to take shape. Once your self-assessment is completed, you should have a clearer understanding of what your strengths are toward creating the business, as well as the gaps that need filling. The character traits you possess will be the core tools for forming a successful business.

It will require a bit of soul searching and a look back at who you are and how you got here. You will learn, as I did, that most people measure up stronger in some quality traits than others. Consider this good news! This knowledge will guide you toward the right people to team up with and will teach you how to plan for a future based on actual, albeit indirectly related, experience. I initially scored high on qualities for salability but fell short on sensibility. Recognizing this over time made all the difference toward my business becoming a successful, growing company as opposed to me just being self-employed. Reading on, you will learn how my personal deficiencies were addressed and transformed into success.

As you have seen, life lessons gleaned from my childhood are highlighted in gray and illustrated to capture the moment. On compiling my recollections, I noted that many ended with something or other being set on fire. This concerned me, as there appeared to be a theme forming that detracted from the main topic: the application of life's lessons to make sound business decisions. I ended up deleting all but a handful of these, along with large portions of the original manuscript, attempting to avoid unnecessary controversy. Nevertheless, I am quite satisfied that ample substance remains intact to achieve what I set out to accomplish. To my sister, Mary Ann, who did her best to protect me, and to my brothers, Hank, Bill, Dick, and Mike, thank you for providing the curricula that ultimately taught me the indispensable principles necessary to succeed in business—and in life.

CHAPTER 1

Laying Out a Future

IN MY EXPERIENCE, IT IS QUITE EASY FOR MOST PEOPLE TO make the decision to start their own business. But actually taking the leap to leave traditional employment and go into business stops most would-be entrepreneurs in their tracks, as though paralyzed by fear. Why is this leap so hard to take? Making the decision to leave a secure job where the responsibility of running the business is left to someone else is no easy thing. If it were, we might all be business owners. This chapter is intended to help those who are truly determined to launch a business build the confidence to make the leap. We'll begin by breaking the leap down into smaller, less intimidating steps. This is where the 4S Assessment comes in. Self-confidence and a determination to succeed are personal qualities common to most successful entrepreneurs and should appear in your 4S Self-assessment, or else there will be a bit more work to do on your part before taking that next step. A bit of advice I give to aspiring business owners is to give your business idea a name so that you begin thinking about it as a real place where you shall soon be working. Once you are satisfied with the name and your vision begins to take shape, acquire a domain name for your business's website and register the name as a legal business entity through either an online service or accountant. These can be accomplished with little effort and expense and while still working for your current employer. Just don't do it on company time! As your actions toward establishing the business gain momentum, so too should your confidence in taking each subsequent step.

For me, the decision to start my own business was an easy one. It was as if it had been thrust upon me with a vengeance. At the time, I had what would appear on paper to be a well-paying, secure job with a good growth trajectory. Another person in my shoes might have missed the subtleties of the situation that drove my decision to leave traditional employment. But to me it was a wakeup call—or wakeup scream to be precise—that I was not meant to be an employee whose destiny was in the hands of others. My lack of business training was supplemented by my wealth of experience—not actual business experience but rather experiences acquired in life, especially during childhood. These experiences shaped my thinking and fertilized my desire to be an entrepreneur. Laying out a future as a business owner under these circumstances was as much a passion as it was a necessity, and now, twenty years later, I'm eager to share the experiences I accumulated with others. This chapter reveals how my personal experiences evolved into a desire to be my own boss and to take full responsibility for whatever came my way. I'll begin by describing the experiences I had and the lessons that accompanied them and how they collectively provided the impetus for the confidence needed to launch my business and, ultimately, to succeed.

My father was employed as an engineer assigned to the metallurgy group at Texas Instruments in Attleboro, Massachusetts.

He was involved in converting the US minted silver quarter to an alloy of 90 percent copper and 10 percent nickel, thereby cutting the material cost to a fraction of its face value. My father was literally making money, so engineering fascinated me even at a young age though I did not act on this inspiration until my mid-twenties. Dad died in an airplane crash when I was nine, so he had little opportunity to offer me career guidance or reinforce my aspirations of being an engineer. This would come later from my brother Hank, who was honorably discharged from military service to help provide for our family after my dad passed away.

Hank had been drafted into the Army during the Vietnam War and soon after his discharge returned to college to join his undrafted buddies, who by then had gained a few semesters on him. He went to Arizona State University in Tempe and encouraged my mother, and the rest of our family, to move out West for a change in scenery. Hank studied electrical engineering and after graduating worked at Motorola until the entrepreneurial itch got the best of him and he bought a television repair shop called Home TV. I had a job in the shop pulling old vacuum tubes from discarded television sets and testing them to see if they were good or bad, then labeling the good ones and putting them in inventory. The repair shop was next door to a bakery, and I would sit testing tubes while eating glazed Long Johns and watching sitcoms on one of the showroom sets. This was as good as it gets for an aimless preteen, and I could not wait to become an engineer myself and open my own TV shop! The only thing standing in the way was a college degree, and it was many years before I drummed up the initiative to enroll.

I began my freshman year in high school at a height of four foot eight inches and weighing all of eighty pounds—a bully's dream. I had inherited the *kick-my-ass* gene. *Curse you, DNA!* My larger high school counterparts were all too eager to exercise upon me their evolutionary responsibility, which Darwin dubbed "Survival of the Fittest." Thank goodness I could run like an Olympic finalist. My brother Dick was a senior in the same school during this time, and one might think having an older brother around would confer upon me some measure of protection. If delaminating my school ID to replace the photo with a sketch of Adolf Hitler was protection, then I had a surplus of it. When I presented my ID at the student bookstore, it was confiscated by a librarian who saw no humor in it, requiring me to purchase a duplicate. The duplicate ID cost ten dollars, the equivalent of ten school lunches, which I had to go without for two weeks.

This was the early '70s when bullying was still in fashion, so the shrewd thing to do was keep a low profile—so low in fact that I went underground, publishing a clandestine newspaper, *The Dibbsville Daily*, with two classmates. It was a sophisticated enterprise and included articles, unflattering commentaries, and even a comic section, which generally followed the imagined exploits of faculty in their private lives. It was the stuff students genuinely cared about rather than the current-affairs nonsense reported in daily newspapers or on the evening news. Besides, we were not bound to the facts. In its second semester and at the height of its popularity, the thing came to a hasty and untimely end as a consequence of taking our investigative journalism too far, crossing a line, and exposing the operation.

Here's what happened. One of our comic strips featured an assistant coach who doubled as a shop teacher. It was well known to us students that his style of speaking included epithets both offensive and controversial in nature, more reminiscent of a marine drill sergeant than a high school educator. One day our esteemed teacher/coach delivered a verbal assault on Anchor Butt, as he called him, who was a student he openly judged to be overweight and under-endowed. We captured this shameful exhibition of mentorship in our cartoon, hiding the identities of those involved, teacher included, but not convincingly enough. The error we made was to include "Anchor Butt" as a character, rather than using a pseudo name. The edition made its way into faculty hands. Soon after, I was told by the assistant principal simply to shut it down, which we did.

My stint as editor-in-chief awakened in me an entrepreneurial spirit that has never died—though it may have dozed from time to time. Ever present and prodding me toward something *better*. In a position where I would be in control, but not for the sake of being in control so much as not *being* controlled—not pushed around or exploited by the bullies of the world.

* * *

LIFE LESSON: Early in my "career," meaning childhood, I was quite enterprising, coming up with inventions to change the world and products to become staples in every household. Of course, none of these grand notions ever materialized, but the dream of making a global impact kept driving me forward. One such product was called Sap-Pine-O, pronounced *sap-**PIE**-no*. The idea for Sap-Pine-O came to me during one of our many camping trips in the pine forest behind our house when I observed that nothing was finer than fallen pinecones for getting a campfire going, even on rainy days when the usual incendiary materials would not light and gasoline was not available. Realizing that the pine sap contained within was the key ingredient, I searched for pine trees that were bleeding sap and collected a large quantity in an old, discarded metal teakettle. This was heated on an open fire to a liquid consistency, then poured into used tuna tins and set aside until cooled to a color and texture reminiscent of spun honey. On camping trips thenceforward, I would break out the Sap-Pine-O, which indeed proved to be both an effective fire starter and able to sustain a flame in its own right for a considerable length of time. There was some grumbling from my critical-minded brothers about the amount of smoke it produced, but I countered that this was actually a benefit as smoke kept mosquitoes away. Admittedly, it was not as clean burning as the better-known chafing fuel *Sterno*, but Sap-Pine-O was free and easily harvested. Although the food items we cooked over it, such as marshmallows and hot dogs, received an instant coating of black soot, we consumed them all the same. As any aspiring entrepreneur, I explored other uses for Sap-Pine-O within my household to expand its market. Two uses stood out to me in particular. The first was as a shoe-shining agent. No matter what color or dullness the shoe, Sap-Pine-O put an instant sheen on it. The second was as a hairstyling pomade, intended to compete with a product popular at that time called *Vitalis*. (Why it was "vital" to have your hair look constantly wet and greasy is beyond my understanding, but the stuff could be found in nearly every household.) After combing and parting my hair as desired, I applied a coating of Sap-Pine-O over my head to hold it in place and to give it a shiny gleam. Both were accomplished, especially the holding-in-place aspect, as a brittle yet impenetrable shield formed upon my hair as though it were encapsulated in cured epoxy resin. As such, it could not be removed even with applications of kerosene, and any object that my head came in contact with became part of my coiffure. The adhesive properties of Sap-Pine-O, which I should have investigated more fully, glued my hair to my scalp.

It could not be adequately cut with scissors or trimmer without leaving bald spots interspersed with splotches of plasticized hair. Worst of all, I had to sport this freakish look at school, where it was concluded I suffered from some disease most likely associated with head lice. Sap-Pine-O sales as a hairstyling agent were not to be, and despite its mosquito-repelling, shoe-shining, and fire accelerant benefits, it saw no revenue. The shame of it was that I had already composed a catchy jingle to ensure astronomical sales: *SAP-PINE-OOOOOOO! IT'S THE WAY TO GOOOOOOO! FROM CANADAAAAAAA! TO MEXICOOOOOOO! WOOWOOWOOO!*

MORAL: Even the most brilliant ideas are subject to failing. Do not let this dissuade you from pursuing your dream. The true value exists more in the process of developing your ideas and less so in the result.

* * *

AFTER HIGH SCHOOL, I FLOUNDERED around with no career-oriented direction or purpose and did not blossom professionally until relatively late in life. My initial desire was to be a rock star. I practiced on my drum set with committed determination, performing whenever and wherever an opportunity presented itself. It turned out, however, that those appraising my musical talent saw little in it that might contribute to the art at large, compelling me to pursue other professions that actually paid a wage. This included dishwasher, lumberjack, woodshop apprentice, pizza maker, and even surgical nurse. My pursuits were essentially random, based on nothing more than what presented itself at the moment.

Following half a lifetime of procrastination, I managed to navigate my way to the engineering program of what is now called the University of Massachusetts at Dartmouth. Imagine my disappointment when there was *not one single class* on television repair. My dream of owning a TV shop like Hank was starting to fade, but undeterred, I opted instead to take the microwave engineering class, thinking fixing microwave ovens was the next best thing to fixing televisions. You might expect that anyone as clueless as I would be the last person to succeed at *anything*, let alone founding a high-value, high-tech business. Then one day, sitting in the communications lab, I came upon an exquisite device called an antenna and was utterly mesmerized by it. Contemplating the complex physics invisibly in motion upon its elegant surface had a profound impact on me. To my mind it was the perfect union between art and science. This cleverly constructed device elicited an electrical response that made long-distance wireless communication possible. What could be more important than *that*!? I wanted to understand and design these things in a way the world had never seen.

I am an antenna engineer. That is the answer I give when people ask, "What do you do?" It is a rare profession; most likely you have never met one. In nearly thirty years in this field, I have not met one socially. How is this relevant to the context of this book? It is relevant because it is a Blue Ocean profession. I'm borrowing the term from W. Chan Kim and Renée Mauborgne, authors of *Blue Ocean Strategy*, which explains how success in business comes by tapping untapped market spaces. It occurred to me in college that I should pursue a field that provided a valuable need, appealed to my intellectual curiosity, and equally important, nobody else wanted to do. Antenna Engineer fit all those criteria, a profession *in demand*. One that would allow me a hand on the tiller as I navigated my career through a twisted maze of hidden opportunities and false promises.

* * *

LIFE LESSON: Antenna design is a branch of electrical engineering. I credit my brother Bill for introducing me to the concept of electricity and its practical use in circuit theory. Bill perfected something he called "the electric handshake." I received many of these growing up, and they are not to be forgotten. It was a variation of the "pull my finger" trick, except in Bill's version you shook his hand. In the hand hidden behind Bill's back, he held a live extension cord with its two conducting wires exposed. When you took the proffered hand, he would close upon the live wires with the other, conducting a high-voltage current (*the source*) through himself (*the transmission line*) and into you (*the load*), thereby completing the circuit. The personification of Ohm's Law. It remains a wonder to me that Bill himself was not electrocuted, but by all appearances it didn't affect him at all. You could judge by his nonstop laughter as you crumpled to the ground, pants shat.

MORAL: Understanding the principles of any field is vastly more important than knowing the vocabulary. Language can be taught, but comprehension must be experienced.

* * *

BETWEEN COLLEGE CLASSES, I RAN into one of my professors, who handed me a copy of an article he uncovered describing a new antenna technology for radar. The article itself was of less interest to me than what was inserted in the middle of it—an advertisement for *Seavey Engineering Associates: Antenna Development and Design.* What got me excited was that they were in Cohasset, Massachusetts, a mere one hour north of Middleboro, where I was living at the time. I was one half-semester away from graduating with a master's degree, and up to that point the only employment prospects for an entry-level engineer were at corporations like Raytheon or General Electric, neither of which held much interest for me. But this Seavey Engineering sounded right up my alley. A modest-sized operation focused exclusively on antenna development—and it was local. I typed up my resume, which boasted marginal hands-on experience, and mailed it to their Human Resources department. Three days later I received a phone call from Mr. John Seavey himself, founder and president, saying, "I got your resume. I want you to come work for me. When can you interview?" I interviewed the very next day and got hired at $31K, contingent upon my subsequent graduation. So began my engineering career as an antenna designer.

My entire stint at Seavey Engineering lasted about sixteen years, over which time I received my PhD and got promoted to the position of chief scientist, reporting directly to the president, John Seavey. John and I became quite close over that time, so close that I viewed him as a quasi-father figure. He confided in me things personal, professional, and company related, and an aspiration formed in me to one day succeed John as president and spend my entire professional career at Seavey Engineering. The company had developed a reputation in the industry for solving difficult antenna problems and, on that basis, had been approached by a company in Middleton, Rhode Island, to oversee a team of engineers to design an antenna that would allow SUVs to track and receive DirecTV satellite service on the move. It was a two-plus-year project, so John at first was reluctant to have his star engineer out of the lineup, but the compensation was far too generous to be refused. John eventually acquiesced, and I was assigned technical lead on the project. I was only too happy for the challenge. Every Thursday I would return to the home office and brief John on the project and discuss various business opportunities and other aspects concerning the company. This went on for nearly two years. One day John said to me, "Charlie, going forward I want to confide in you all matters relating to the company and discuss plans for laying out our future." I interpreted this as: "Charlie, get ready to take over. I'm getting ready to retire." This was big news! I was both thrilled and melancholic, realizing that for me to take John's position would mean he was vacating it—and I loved working with him. My mind was racing as I drove to my assignment in Middleton with visions of occupying the president's office and leading the company into the future. Maybe I would start wearing a suit or carry a fancy cane and sport a monocle like those Wall Street moguls of old...Anything was possible, as I soon found out.

***

LIFE LESSON: In 1967, Dick and I got kicked off the school bus for life. He was in the ninth grade; I was in the sixth. Every day getting off the bus, we would each pick up a stone and toss it in the bus's direction as it drove off to the next stop. There was no malice in it whatsoever; it was a simple, mindless gesture conducted in the most leisurely fashion, like chewing on a straw of grass or whittling a piece of wood. We never intended to hit the bus, so when the back window shattered into a thousand beads, revealing an astonished passenger in the rearmost seat, whose framed face was a living portrayal of Edvard Munch's *The Scream*, we were frozen in disbelief. We immediately thawed from this spell when our bus driver exited the bus on a dead run. The poor man was vertically challenged and had to wear special boots to reach the foot pedals, so he may well have caught us if not for the six-inch lifts he sported. He finally gave up the chase and returned to the bus occupants he'd quickly abandoned to pursue us. We thought he might drive back to our house, but he did not, clearly not so committed to delivering the shouted threats he promised at our retreat. Rather than inform our mother of the incident, let alone face the bus driver, we thenceforward walked the six miles to and home from school. This went on nearly three weeks until a revision to our route gave us away. To shorten our daily trek, we started leaving the main road to cross a field and ford a shallow stream, shaving off thirty minutes. This meant getting wet, and my mother, being observant and in charge of laundry, caught on. Our explanation did not include breaking a bus window, so in her ignorance of the facts she simply insisted we take the bus instead of walking. As we waited at our stop, the bus flew by, accelerating as it did so. We reported this to our mother, feigning no understanding of the driver's irrational behavior, which our mother then reported to the school principal. The cause of our eviction was soon revealed, and our "the tire must have hit a rock that popped up..." defense gained no traction. There was to be no acquittal, forcing us to accept the consequences of our complacent rock-tossing. To this day, I think I threw the fatal stone, and Dick thinks he threw it. We will never know, and that is exactly as it should be.

MORAL: When setting goals, be sensible of what you aim for because what appears certain can turn volatile unexpectedly—and rapidly.

* * *

AFTER MY MEETING WITH JOHN, a lab technician I worked with in Middleton said to me, "I hear Seavey Engineering is for sale." I laughed out loud and asked what ever gave him that idea. He said the program manager told him. I asked the program manager, and she confirmed it, saying the CEO had told her. How could this be? I had been sitting in John's office not two hours before, and he'd said nothing of selling. Instead, I was hearing it from a technician who worked at another company out of state? I immediately called John, who seemed more concerned about the breach in confidentiality than the betrayal I was feeling. He told me during that call he was NOT selling the company, which I already knew was not true. It was all a shock to me. I recall nothing more of that conversation, if there was any. I later learned the company was not only for sale but had been for some time. Out of a field of ten potential buyers, one had already been selected, and the process of conducting due diligence, examining financials, product catalog, customer base, and whatnot, had begun. Much later, after everything had unfolded, John told me he got the bad advice not to disclose this information to employees for fear of a mass exodus. So that summed up my relationship with him. Anything more was disillusionment on my part. He did not tell me the truth for fear I might do exactly what I ended up doing—because he did *not* tell me the truth. I respect that an owner has every right to sell their company, but making decisions that do not consider, let alone acknowledge, the culture that exists within the workforce is just plain stupid. To succeed in business, it helps to recognize stupidity when it emerges in your path and steer clear of it. Steering is the easy part. Recognizing, not so much.

The new owner, Pradeep, was president and part owner of another antenna company, so this was to be a merger/acquisition. It turned out to be a murder/suicide. I did not return to the home office during the transition period that followed, opting instead to work remotely at my assignment in Middleton. In time Pradeep called to let me know he had taken up residency in John's office as the new president and wanted to meet and discuss next steps concerning my relationship with the company. Ever the optimist, I was thinking he would surely recognize my contributions and reward me with an enormous bonus, a raise, a new title, shares in ownership, whatever it took to keep an *essential* employee on the payroll.

After listening to Pradeep speak for about five minutes, I understood two things: (1) he did not give a shit about antennas and (2) he did not give a shit about me. Then he announced that he was reducing my salary by $20K. NON-NEGOTIABLE. He explained that the company was barely making a profit, so he was cutting back salaries and dropping all products that did not carry a certain minimum margin, no matter who relied on them. I told him I would consider all this new information, and we agreed to meet the following week. In truth, my mind had already been made up. It was clear to me that this sort of thinking would not make for a *sustainable* relationship, and my good *sensibilities* kicked in and told me to get the hell out. The way I saw it, he was blaming and punishing the loyal, hardworking employees for the company's lack of profitability. This was stupid, and I needed to steer clear of it. The only shred of positive feeling I received after departing that joyless encounter was the hint of doubt that registered on his face when it appeared to him as though I might decline his offer. Although neither he nor I appreciated it at the time, my departure/dismissal would eventually set in motion the decline of once-heralded Seavey Engineering by delivering a serious blow to its future *scalability*.

The week that followed was one of the busiest in my life. Before leaving my meeting with Pradeep, I informed the HR manager that I would be taking the upcoming week off as vacation time, off the clock as they say. I had neither an employee contract nor a noncompete agreement to bind me, so I busied myself calling friends, colleagues, and potential customers in the industry. This was essentially cold calling, something I ordinarily despise but a necessity if I was to succeed at building a business from ground level. It was also a self-test of my salability to the industry, bringing me a sense of optimism and confidence to proceed. I also engaged a lawyer to help me set up and establish the new business and to discuss options for recouping the nearly $100K Seavey Engineering owed me for unpaid travel expenses, offsite salary differential, and other compensation for which I had a written agreement. (*Pradeep later refused to honor the agreement as it was not made by him.* This meant I would have to sue John, which my lawyer was eager to undertake, for a portion of the settlement.)

The other thing I did over that week was speak to several potential employees and an eventual partner, Greg, whom I met at the Middleton development project. Greg agreed to join me in my new venture, which I had incorporated under the name Micro-Ant, Inc., once it got rolling. Satisfied that the necessary elements were in place to establish and sustain a small, emerging business, I told my wife, Laurie, about the plan. Laurie's greatest attribute is also her biggest flaw: she believes in me implicitly and without reservation. Rats! I had half-hoped she would talk me out of it. But instead, she saw what I was going through and simply said she would work double shifts if needed until Micro-Ant got off the ground. Now I had a plan, and if it didn't work, no matter. It would be better to work as a ditch digger under my own terms than as a chief scientist for a corporate *bully* who valued me only so far as he could exploit me. It was a plan that contemplated only success because it was designed to achieve my primary objective, which was to be free of corporate manipulation.

* * *

LIFE LESSON: Years ago, we kept a dog kennel behind the house, where our family raised purebred beagles. My chores included feeding them and cleaning the enclosed walking areas. One day I stood leaning with my face pressed against the wire fence, singing a fine rendition of "Donkey Chain" by Wayne Newton. As I opened my mouth wide to hit a difficult note, one of the beagles—Honey was her name—did one of those stretches dogs do and kicked up her rear leg, projecting a piece of dog shit into my mouth. My first instinct was to spit it out, but because it was still fresh, my tongue would not roll the foul projectile into a tangible object that could be expelled. I ran back to the house crying, brown drool exiting my half-open mouth and hanging from my chin. On the way, I passed Dick, who asked what was wrong. "I haff daw shiff in my mouff," I said, finding it difficult to form hard consonants. Dick responded casually, "You're going to die. That stuff's poisonous." I continued into the house to find my mother in the kitchen. She was more sympathetic to my plight. She washed my mouth out, gave me a glass of milk, and told me it was the antidote to every poison, which eased my fear of dying and which I believed for many, many years.

> **MORAL:** When a plan runs afoul and threatens your livelihood, STOP. Most likely, you are looking at things the wrong way. View it as an opportunity and respond so that the outcome is in your favor. Become the victor, not the victim.

* * *

I RETURNED TO PRADEEP'S OFFICE for the appointed meeting with a wide grin, which he mistook as acquiescence to the "proposal" he imposed the week before. He glided across the floor like a ballroom dancer eager to waltz, hand proffered, which I took and shook. It was an electric handshake, and he was the load. Looking him in the eyes, both our faces beaming, I said precisely, "This is my last day. I am done. Good luck with your company." As I turned to leave the office, he said something. It may have been "Wait," but I did not oblige. Instead I continued, unemployed and excited at whatever the future should bring. There was much more that could have been said and possibly should have been said, but likely all conversation from that point on would have been eloquent of derision.

When others seek my advice on starting up their own business, I ask them how much work they would need booked before feeling secure enough to leave their job. Typically, the answer has been several months to a year, sometimes more, sometimes less. I tell them to forget it. Two weeks. If your threshold is more than two weeks, you don't have the determination or self-assuredness necessary to take on the risk that goes with being independently employed. I walked away from Seavey

Engineering with less than two weeks of *potential* work but a burning desire to put those people (and all of corporate America for that matter) in the rear-view mirror. At that point I did not care if I ended up shoveling shit for a living so long as I was doing it on my own terms. That pretty much summed up my contingency plan.

In this chapter, I've described the circumstances surrounding my transition from employee to future employer. I took the leap because I wanted to be my own boss—but also because I didn't want to be someone else's tool. With these two notions aligned in my head, the decision to head off on my own was a simple one. Because I'd faced situations during childhood not all that different from the encounter with my now ex-employer, the path to take was not difficult to see. Electric handshakes and dog shit in the mouth may not be in your personal repertoire, but I assure you there are similar experiences in your life that can provide guidance as you navigate the transition from employee to employer. Imagine the fateful day when you break loose and embark on your new career as entrepreneur and how that encounter might evolve. Now think back to other experiences in your life, especially those that were uncomfortable or even downright devastating. How they turned out at the time is less important than what they mean to you now and what lessons can be extracted from them that can aid you in a similar encounter going forward. Most of us do this intuitively, but I'm suggesting you do this as a formal exercise. Write down a condensed version of the event, just as I have written my Life Lessons, and develop a moral for each as though your intent was to guide another person facing a similar situation. Here's a hint: the person you are guiding is you. There may be a lot more to these past experiences than you give them credit for, and in them you will discover character traits upon which a successful business is founded. You may well discover in this exercise the confidence to enter uncertain water and the wisdom to navigate through it.

CHAPTER 2

Developing Partnerships

THERE IS NO SUCH THING AS A SOLO CAREER. EVEN A SOLOIST must rely on the support of many others to perform, including the customers that form the audience attending the performance. The world around you is populated by people who will be essential to the success of your business, as either employees, vendors, customers, or advisors. There is no hierarchy to these relationships; they are all vital in their own way. Regardless of what roles each may play, they are all partners in your business once you bring them into your sphere. The relationships with these partners and how you manage them will largely determine the sustainability and scalability of your operation. Remember, until you have sustainability, you are not truly a business, and scalability is what facilitates growth. During the beginning stages of your business, you need to establish relationships and treat them as the essential assets they are. I had many friends in the industry on both the supplier and customer side even before launching Micro-Ant, many of whom contributed in no small way to my success. Some also became future employees, and some became partners in ownership. But the very first relationship I called upon was the one with my brother Dick, who acted as an advisor—though the advice was sometimes obscure.

Amid writing up a business plan, creating a website, printing my own business cards, and all those tasks associated with establishing a business, I sought the advice of my brother Dick. Confidentially, I needed his permission to sign over ownership of the boat we jointly owned to my attorney, who'd agreed to take it as payment toward services mentioned earlier. Out of six siblings, Dick is by far the smartest, but his tendency to weave arid-dry humor into almost everything he says results in advice that turns out to be either exceptionally good or incredibly bad. You never know if what he is telling you is serious or a setup for one hell of a broom-goosing.

Dick had two pieces of advice for me. The first was to drop the suit against Seavey, that it would be a distraction when my attention toward the business would be needed the most, and that any money awarded would taint my good years of service to the company. He said I should leave "squeaky clean." That was very good advice. His second nugget of advice was that I rename my new company KrapAss Industries. First, because the "K" would make it look German, and everyone knows Germans are the best engineers. Second, people don't forget a name like KrapAss, and it would be instantly popular. He felt strongly enough about it to paint KrapAss Industries in bold font on the wall of a test chamber I subsequently built in my mother's barn. As provocative as KrapAss Industries sounded, I opted instead to stick with Micro-Ant, which is short for **Micro**wave **Ant**ennas. (The hyphen is there because the domain name for the non-hyphenated version, MicroAnt, was already taken.) Also, I imagined the search words that would lead an online browser to a website called KrapAss would likely not be intended to find antennas.

A few months after operations began, KrapAss was not looking like all that bad a name, as many assumed Micro-Ant meant to imply micro or miniature antennas. Maybe it affected business in the early days by diverting away customers looking for normal-sized antennas, but in time it became recognized as the industry standard for quality antenna products.

In July of 2003, I set up an office in the basement of our home sufficient for conducting a business based on consulting services, with a computer and a phone representing the extent of my corporate assets. I was way too busy to be lonely, even though the first employee would not start until after the new year. Greg was still employed in Middleton but did some moonlighting on Micro-Ant's behalf, contributing to the trickling revenue stream that would be critical to launching the company. He too would give notice to his employer and come on board full time after the new year. As it so happened, when Greg quit his job, his former CEO sent me a nasty letter replete with accusations, threats, and promised consequences. Incidentally, this was the same CEO who violated Seavey Engineering's NDA, which stipulated not to disclose the company was up for sale, and who also attempted to poach me away from John Seavey during my assignment on his project. The letter was so wonderfully crafted it is a shame I have misplaced it and cannot reprint it here so that we might all share in its inspirational message. Upon receiving it I was concerned not a little by the legal jargon it contained as it was certainly written by an attorney and cited the countless laws I had breached. I showed Dick the letter, seeking his advice on what steps to take before contacting my own attorney. Dick studied it carefully, contemplating it judiciously, and then succinctly offered his guidance: "Frame it. This is your first recognition of being a legitimate business." That was the last I heard on the matter, so apparently Dick's advice was spot on.

Being a one-person operation at this stage was a necessity because the only cash I had on hand was my dwindling 401k and about $50K in promissory notes, which in total was still not sufficient to support a payroll. A promissory note is where you go to your friends and family and beg them for money, any that they are willing to give, in exchange for a written promise to pay it back with interest within some agreed-upon term. As in life, many of the actions we take in business are based on faith. Faith that the other party we are dealing with is being honest and truthful and has the wherewithal to execute that part of the transaction for which they are responsible. This is what the phrase "acting in good faith" is meant to imply. If someone tells you that they intend to purchase something from you, then you have to make a choice whether to begin execution immediately or to delay this service until money has changed hands. A number of elements go into this decision, such as the credentials of the individual you're dealing with, your history with them, a credit check of their finances...but ultimately it comes down to your faith in them, just as it comes down to their faith in you and your ability to execute. When it comes to borrowing money, faith is typically not a consideration with most lenders, unless those lenders happen to be your family or close friends, who are often willing to operate on blind faith. Lending institutions do not make risky loans. They first want to establish your wherewithal to pay back the loan or else establish sufficient collateral in the event you don't.

My promise was to pay back these notes within five years at a cumulative interest of prime plus two percent, a decent return at the time. It's a great way to raise capital when no one else in their right mind would lend you any, and the terms are more favorable to the borrower than a conventional or venture capital (VC) loan. For instance, your mother-in-law is far less likely to demand collateral or foreclose on your home in the event of a default than a bank might be. Equally important, you retain ownership of your company; you don't have to turn over a controlling interest to a trusted family friend as you would a venture capitalist or angel investor.

We paid off these notes within a year, which registered a degree of disappointment amongst a couple of our benefactors. One told me that they were disappointed because they hoped we would default, allowing them to convert their note into shares in ownership. They believed even then that it would be the best long-term investment available for the money. They were correct; a rough calculation indicates that their return would have been over one thousand times their original investment ten years after the investment if it had converted to Micro-Ant stock. I'm no math wizard, but my partner Jim taught me that one thousand times anything is a thousand times bigger and easy to calculate. The prudent thing to do is retain ownership *and* control or else lose the value and self-direction that got you motivated in the first place.

***

LIFE LESSON: One year we were snowed in by a two-day blizzard and going stir crazy. To pass the time, we invented a game that required wading out into the deep snow, barefoot, carrying a red checkered washrag, and dropping it. Each contestant in turn would follow the footprints to the rag and advance it. The game continued for some time, the rag getting farther and farther away. Mike was hanging on much longer than Dick or I anticipated. Just after Mike had begun his latest run, our mother asked us to let the two dogs out to do their business and get fresh air. We did so and then waited for Mike's return, which turned into many minutes, causing us concern. As we opened the door to begin our search, there was Mike carrying the rag, panting and crying, near collapse, feet beet red with the dogs dancing around him. He explained that they overtook him, grabbed the rag after he advanced it, and headed off into the woods, joining in on the fun. We later retraced Mike's steps as he'd chased the dogs. His determination was impressive; he'd even crossed the railroad tracks. It was difficult to declare Mike the loser, especially as he lay on the floor crying and in the throes of frostbite, the dogs licking the ice off his face and he still clutching the rag—and his dignity. He could have simply run back to the house claiming that he'd fulfilled his obligation to move the rag and that the dogs had done what dogs do, which was wholly out of his control. But dammit, it was his turn, his rag, his pride, and come hell or high snow nobody was taking that away.

MORAL: Beware of the dogs in the corporate woods waiting to fleece you. Don't let them take ownership of what is rightfully yours.

* * *

COME NOVEMBER 2003 WE HAD as much consulting work as two could handle, and our fledgling company was gaining steam. We did two journal interviews to get our name out, resulting in even more business, but there were only so many hours in a day that two can bill for. Our revenue cap was severely limited. To make money, real money, we either needed to add a bevy of consultants or provide finished goods. We won a small production order, and like a one-man-operation, I personally undertook every task from design to fabrication to boxing and shipping. It was a fine success and taught me, more than anything else, that I did not want to ever do that again on my own. From the proceeds of sales such as this, I brought on Rob to manage operations. Rob was one of many who defected after the Seavey acquisition, and he played a major role in setting up our infrastructure and various departments. It seemed funny that we had four times as many departments as employees, but we were bent on success and planning for the future. We kept a white board, which changed almost weekly and indicated that in some operations I reported to Rob and in others he reported to me. It seems somewhat convoluted thinking about it now, but it was our first critical undertaking toward sustainability.

The nature of our business in its early stages was such that there was little need or value in having a marketing department in the conventional sense. Each time we engaged sales reps, the results never benefited us, so we put an end to outside marketing. The same was true of our website; it produced little to no business. It was simply there as a point of reference and to supply contact information for potential customers. The quality of our website was so poor even KrapAss Industries would be ashamed of it, and it was nearly twenty years before we brought it up to a standard commensurate with our reputation in the industry. This is because we were not building a catalog of products that customers could pick and choose from. Rather, we were selling technology that took the form of unique products, each intended for a specific customer. The concept raised concern with some of our employees who were accustomed to working in organizations with large marketing groups. An employee responsible for overseeing our financial accounting often worried at our lack of hard data for forecasting revenue in the upcoming year. Finally, unable to contain herself, she blurted out, "Where is our business going to come from!?" I answered, pointing through a window, "Out there." It's not that I was operating on faith so much as confidence in our strategy and the plan we had in place to succeed. Such was my attitude toward developing business, and we suffered little from it. My point was that the business would come so long as we built a solid organization to execute it when it did. That, and make sure we had something unique and valuable to offer in the transaction. If I was operating on faith, it was in the value of our technology, which I trusted unconditionally.

* * *

LIFE LESSON: At the time of this lesson there were two houses on our property. One was a three-bedroom shack in which our family of eight dwelled for many years until my dad earned enough to build a new accommodation for us. We forever referred to the original home as the old house and the new home, you guessed it, as the new house. During construction of the new house, my Aunt Gertie and Uncle Frankie left their home in Boston and purchased the property across the street from us, building themselves a new home as well. Aunt Gertie was an industrious sort, constantly tending the fifty acres she owned by trimming trees, building rock gardens, and such. Often, she would use the stone fireplace in the old house, which still functioned, to dispose of the unwanted brush she collected. Mike and I knew where bullets were kept for various rifles my dad had, and we secured the largest shell, tossed it into the raging fireplace, and ran outside. As we exited, we met Aunt Gertie entering with a load of brush. We told her not to go in there. She asked why. We told her there *might* be a bullet in the fire. She asked why there would be a bullet in the fire. We replied we did not know, but there *might* be. She entered despite our warning. Judging her to be irrational to our logic, Mike and I set off to put as much distance between us and the fireplace as possible before the impending explosion. The sound produced by the bullet was quite impressive; it created an echo that rang through the woods. Yet the sound that left an everlasting impression upon us was Aunt Gertie's shrill cry of "MARY!"—my mother's name. She could well have been summoning the Divine Mother, but we did not hang around to ask which of the two we should be running from.

MORAL: Successful deals do not need elaborate selling, nor do they need to rely on Hail Marys. Shape your business such that reliable products and excellent customer service do the marketing for you.

* * *

THE NO-MARKETING STRATEGY LIKELY SOUNDS ridiculous to you, but hear me out. I do not contend that this will work for all businesses, but I am also not interested in all businesses. My interest is toward those that offer a product or service that is provided in a way that is unique and without competition. Let's review my circumstances after leaving Seavey Engineering. I started a company doing the exact same thing as the company I had just left. A one-man operation with zero credit and marginal credibility up against one of the top antenna design firms in the free world. They had a well-distributed catalog both in print and online with hundreds of legacy products developed over a period of three decades. They operated in a hundred-thousand-square-foot state-of-the-art manufacturing facility boasting impressive assets and human resources. I was a single-person operation secluded in a basement lately occupied by two dogs. Seavey was the lion and I the mouse struggling to survive by attempting to eat their lunch crumbs. My strategy was a simple one. Instead of developing products that we could sell to a lot of customers, we would develop a modest list of customers that we could sell a lot of products to.

Those in the business of appraising companies such as ours would view this as a "concentration risk," meaning we had too many eggs in one basket and should be more diverse in our customer portfolio. In this case, they would be wrong. This is, in truth, a "concentration benefit" because it means that choice companies commanding a substantial portion of their industry's market are utterly reliant on us to satisfy their product demand with no competition for us. Each of these opportunities evolves into a long-term partnership that is sustained by our upstanding reputation of delivering good products on good terms. To ensure we adhered to this model, I devised a project code system that named each product after the customer it was developed for. The customer ended up getting a product unique to them, which we would sell to no one else, least of all their competitors, and we in turn developed a customer who was obliged to satisfy their unique requirement by buying exclusively from us. When a potential customer approaches us, we make it clear that if they expect us to compete against another designer/supplier or if their requirement can be satisfied by an existing product, we respectfully decline the opportunity.

We do not fret over passing up these opportunities because if the requirement is a commodity or otherwise not unique, then we'd be left competing on price alone and needlessly giving up profit margin. As I like to say, if it's not an oddity, it's a commodity. If the opportunity *is* unique, then we feel pretty confident about it being awarded to us. If at first they don't like our terms or the cut of our jib, they'll be back. Why? Because they generally have only two other options: (1) engage their own internal designers (if they have any) or (2) engage a designer/supplier who is too focused on developing a product catalog to acquire the technical depth necessary to solve their unique problem. Clearly option one is unlikely to succeed for them or else they wouldn't have been outsourcing the job in the first place. Option two, though, poses a special problem. In one scenario, the designer/supplier is engaged and successfully completes the job, the champagne is uncorked, and everyone is happy. In scenario two, the designer/supplier is engaged and remains engaged until all the money, time, and hope have been expended with little to show for it other than a bucket of miscellaneous parts. Now the customer returns to us, desperate, out of money, and out of time. Once we solve their problem, we have another customer for life added to our portfolio. If we were to list all the customers that came to us after having engaged other designers/suppliers (including Seavey Engineering, who defaulted on their projects), it would fill a catalog.

Jim, our CEO, says it best: "The company views itself as a thread inextricably woven into the fabric of an enterprise that involves vendors, customers, employees, and owners. Decisions that affect one stakeholder affect all stakeholders. The company believes that its decisions and behavior are critical to the maintenance of the fabric of the entire enterprise. The company avoids doing business with companies that hold a view that business is a zero-sum game." Essentially, the success of any enterprise relies upon the relationships shared amongst and between the entities participating within it. Choose your vendors as you would your employees. But choose your customers? Yes, or at least manage the relationship so that it fosters good business transactions. Our philosophy has always been never to compete on price alone. If a customer approaches us with a product that could be obtained elsewhere, we simply point them to it. All our products are custom to a specific customer and to a specific application. We are engaged because the customer is looking for something unique that gives them a technical advantage over their competitors. It is a good strategy that works because they are buying a product that can only be purchased from us, making our business an essential component in their business plan. But never take advantage of it! Your success is bound to theirs, so treat that relationship with utter respect and fairness.

Another concern in our case is that our biggest competitors are the very customers that engage us—the ones that retain departments with resource capability sufficient to achieve their needs. But many have grown into an edifice of bureaucracy that cannot effectively tap into its own resources, finding it far more cost effective and expedient to outsource. As you might imagine, this presents somewhat of a dilemma. What prevents them from taking and producing our technology, cutting us out of the supply chain? Only the strength of our relationship and the integrity of the customer. It's not any contract or agreement promising not to do so. These are easily circumvented whereas a strong relationship is ironclad. Have we ever had customers misappropriate our intellectual property despite agreeing contractually not to do so? You bet! But we are a small company and not in the business of litigation. It's expensive, distracting, and yields little benefit in the long term. Our only course of action is recognizing that company for the bully they are and putting them on the Non-Approved Customer list. The KrapAss list.

* * *

OVER THE NEXT FEW MONTHS, Rob, Greg, and I continued to build the business, filling various positions that the company needed for growth. The most important choices you make in business generally involve who you bring on. The best and worst decisions we made were with respect to who we hired. The thing is, everyone looks pretty good on paper, but you have no idea how they will affect the organization until they are neck deep in it. Once you've established that an applicant has the skills necessary to perform the job, it's time to take a deeper dive into what personal traits they possess to determine how they will mesh with your company culture. What I've learned while interviewing candidates is to focus on three key traits:

- *Intelligence*

- *Work ethic*

- *Submission to authority*

Experience is secondary to these. Anyone can gain experience over time, but attributes like intelligence and personal character are innate and cannot be taught. Why is submitting to authority important? The reason is, like it or not, a successful business is a dictatorship, not a democracy. Companies that make decisions based on committee tend to be sluggish and inefficient. Strong leadership is tantamount to having a strong and successful business. Employees who defy leadership in favor of acting in a self-serving manner create information silos and consternation. If they do not respect authority, they will not respect the objectives or the processes in place to achieve them, leading to *dis*organization as opposed to organization. Without organization there is no team, no sustainability, no company. An organization chart (Org chart) must be established that identifies the chain of leadership and operations starting with the executive office and extending throughout. The Org chart is an important component in the overall corporate strategy and is the human factor that brings a company to life, making it sustainable and scalable. To be positive-minded contributors, employees must be clear on who they report to and what they are responsible for. Keep in mind that you will be spending most of your waking hours with these people, especially during the early stages of growing the business, so having good relationships with open communication is crucial to building a team with a common goal. Remember, these may be the people who lead your company in the future, so choose well.

Each time you add a new member to the team, you should strive also to add *depth* to the organization. Adding depth means creating a capability overlap within the workforce in addition to supplementing your institutional knowledge. It also means you are contributing to the 4S pool, bringing more sensibility and especially sustainability into the company toolbox. A critical operation dependent upon a specific individual puts the company at risk, especially if that individual takes an extended leave of absence. Think of it: an entire portion of the business comes to a halt until that person returns to duty or a replacement is found. All the better if that replacement, even if temporary, is already on the work force and ready to step in. Antenna design is a rare commodity, so Greg and I would split the development jobs but keep ourselves updated on each other's progress in case one of us was unavailable and the other had to fill in. If your business relies on mowing grass, make sure you have two mowers—the machine and the operator. We continue to practice overlap in everything we do to avoid the risk of an operational blackout and to ensure our sustainability.

* * *

LIFE LESSON: My mother was a fabulous cook. She would preserve her own fruits and vegetables, bake bread and desserts from scratch (including the wonderful whoopie pie), brew root beer, and prepare the entire Italian haute cuisine from memory. You might think with that level of culinary mastery on hand mealtime would be a delight. Alas, not for me. It appeared to me that Ma had a gift for serving dishes to make me gag. In her defense, I did not like any food growing up and cannot recall ever finishing an entire meal. Instead, I adopted several survival techniques such as hiding bits of food in my drink, pant cuffs, shirt pocket, or any other compartment where it might go undetected and later be discharged outdoors. Worse, my brothers made sport by counting out loud in unison how many times it took me to chew a particular morsel, with wagers exchanged on how many chews would precede a swallow. One day

I discovered a hole in the wall to one side of the refrigerator where an electrical outlet was meant to be installed. This new, hidden wall space allowed scalability to my food disposal operation and greatly reduced my transportation cost of sneaking outside. It became my dumping ground when no one was looking, allowing the disposal of large portions all at once, as opposed to tiny bits here and there. The mice dealt with this offal so far as I knew, but if so, they were not able to keep up with my prodigious production rate. This forced me to fling food sideways into the deeper recesses of the wall. One morning my mother fixed me scrambled eggs, knowing full well I hated the stuff, which incited me to dispose of it in the usual manner. I executed a most ambitious fling for good measure. All was good until two days later when my mother marched upstairs from the cellar carrying the spoiled eggs in a towel and thrust them into my mouth. My fling had sent the food through a hole in the floor onto a drainpipe located above the washing machine in our basement, where my mother discovered it Adding to my anguish, Dick and his friend CT appeared and pretended to be sports commentators, remarking on what an *eggs-asperating eggs-perience* this was and the like. Truth is, they tasted no worse than the first go-around, and there were less of them too. My mother possessed cooking skills rivaling any chef's, and here I was eating rotten eggs.

> **MORAL:** Skill is only as valuable as how it is managed and employed.

* * *

BUILDING A GREAT TEAM IS the most rewarding aspect of owning a business. Your employees will inspire you to hold your own bar high and higher. They are trusting you with their livelihoods, and we owe it as managers to acknowledge their dedication and make decisions that safeguard their well-being. It is incumbent upon owners and managers to provide employees a workplace environment that encourages personal and professional prosperity. The risk of permitting even a single obstacle to stand in the way unchecked is a breach of that oath. Deal with all such issues decisively and always toward preserving the fabric of the organization.

Many companies struggle with being correct versus being right. Being correct tends to favor a single individual or a select group of individuals, whereas being right works in the interest of the entire organization. It's a delicate subject and one not easy to address without being politically *incorrect*. "Right" is binary whereas "correct" comes in many shades. *(Dick once told me two wrongs don't make a right, which is easily proved using Boolean algebra)*. To illustrate, suppose you have an employee on staff who simply does not fit in. Maybe they lack capability or work ethic or display behaviors that do not blend well with the company culture. The *correct* thing to do is find or create another job within the organization that suits them better, to relocate them within the workflow, and to minimize further disruption. Alternatively, the *right* thing to do is immediately discharge them for their own good and for the good of the company. This is what Jack Welch, ex-chairman and CEO of GE, would recommend. Instead, we tend to invoke kindness and other emotions into our decision-making, often at great expense and detriment to the organization. We are not the wolf pack (*or Jack Welch*) that only does the *right* thing. When a member of the pack proves unfit to keep up, it is discharged from the group or dispatched by more permanent means. We are human after all, and survival has a different meaning for us. But a true act of kindness is one that prevents prolonged suffering of an ill-fitting employee and of those left to pick up the slack. It means doing the right thing *correctly*. Don't delay a decision once the need to act has become publicly obvious; it detracts from doing the right thing. It is important to find the proper balance between correctness and rightness in our decision-making. Each decision affects the entire organization at many levels. Lean toward those benefiting the greater good.

Despite your best efforts, you may still find yourself with an ill-fitting employee who is simply recalcitrant and rejects the corporate philosophy. This can become a source of stress, disruption, or even paralysis. They might possess over-the-top intelligence yet display a subpar work ethic or, worse, be passively antagonistic toward authority. Authority refers not only to the hierarchy established by the company's organizational chart but also its policies and moral code. Most frustrating is that these individuals may well have abilities exceeding all others or the potential to be your greatest asset, but some character flaw makes them unreliable or prone to behaviors serving their own purpose and opposed to the interests of the company at large. Most authors of business management books will advise us to discharge these individuals expeditiously to avoid a toxic situation and before everyone else gets a sip of the poison. That may be the *right* thing, but the reality is that it might *not* be the *correct* course of action for various reasons. Maybe that employee has trade secret knowledge that could be used against the company. Maybe Uncle Leo will call in his loan if Junior is let go, causing you to file for bankruptcy. Or maybe the employee has skills vital to the operation that are not easily replaced. I lacked the authority to discharge my mother as the household cook. Even if I'd had it, starving to death was not an attractive alternative, so I *correctly* managed otherwise.

Managing to succeed is simple enough so long as you have the right people with the right attitudes, but quite complicated if even one individual on the team is in discord with the corporate agenda. What is to be done in that case? You must contain the situation as though invoking quarantine. In the context of medical remediation, a quarantine is used to isolate an infected individual or small population from the general population to prevent the spread of contamination. A quarantine is not meant to be permanent; once the situation is resolved, it's back to business as usual. This is a good analogy for the case in business when you have a particular individual, small group, or situation that will have a potentially negative effect on the entire organization if allowed to continue unchecked. Establish a virtual boundary to isolate the company culture from individuals or elements that might inadvertently create conflict. Within the boundaries of that imagined compartment, assign specific goals that must be met and a semi-rigid timeline. What is most important is that the sole responsibility of the undertaking is clearly defined to the insubordinate individual. Quarantines are not time restricted; they take as long as they take. If it never gets done? Lower the bar. This is a process that may sometimes be necessary to keep both the work and the difficult employee moving in the right direction. Adapt by reducing assignment complexity until achievement is certain. Do not let this individual's responsibility prematurely transfer beyond the imagined boundary in a manner that hinders company resources or fires up the blame machine. Contain responsibility until it produces the desired result before evolving into the next phase of the workflow process. Granted, it seems like a lot of effort, but it's a necessary course of action when termination is simply not a simple option. Speaking from experience, it is the only method that facilitates a positive outcome in even the most dire of circumstances or when all other options seem untenable. Threats, reprimands, and "constructive feedback" tend to breed resentment and more insubordination. De-personalize the situation and deal with it objectively. It is a process meant to be the opposite of termination; it's built instead upon *de*-termination and places the onus upon the manager to make it succeed.

The following describes a situation that evolved over time into an HR nightmare but was dealt with in the manner just described. It is our policy to employ the best-suited person for the job, based on qualifications, attitude, and character, to which we credit our remarkably collegial, diverse, and capable workforce. We hired a highly qualified individual possessing these attributes and tasked them with establishing a new department within the company, giving them liberal reign to do so, including the hiring of all pertinent positions. As people were brought on and the department grew, questions were raised within the organization about the competency of these individuals as evidently this team was doing the opposite of what it was commissioned for. Instead of expediting product flow, it was bringing it to a complete halt, and much discussion within the employee ranks centered on how incapable this department was of understanding or handling what was expected of them. It was obvious they were being hired based on attributes other than competency. There was no denying it; they were being hired primarily based on skin color. Relative to every other department within the company, this one department had the least diversity by far. We had an acknowledged racist in our midst, an HR nightmare that ran contrary to our practice of celebrating diversity and of choosing the most qualified person for the job. The situation was poison to our culture, so one of my first initiatives after assuming the role of president was to tackle this problem.

Putting yourself in my position, what would you do? Better yet, what would fairness and ethical behavior *demand* that you do? Hell, what would the law *require* that you do? If terminating the head and/or the entire department was your answer, forget it. Just imagine the discrimination lawsuits that would be filed. You'd have little hope of a convincing defense in a climate where the mere utterance of a person's ethnicity, persuasion, or political leaning in any context is PR doom for every employer. Although this was clearly a case of discrimination, we had to tread carefully or else be accused of the very thing we were trying to eradicate. We began by reassigning each team member to other departments and had their team leader report directly to me. I spent hours and hours coaching and assigning that person tasks that were simple and intended to promote diversity and success. In the end, every individual originating from that department, including the head manager, quit of their own accord, save one who developed into a superstar once given the opportunity of working under a caring, open-minded manager, exemplifying the power in quality relationships.

***

LIFE LESSON: Mike had a newspaper route making deliveries on his bicycle. I had my driver's license and, always in need of gas money, offered to drive Mike on the route for half his pay plus the cost of gas. He had ample customers to make it worthwhile, and it was all quite simple and pleasant, save for one customer, Ruth G. This woman complained to newspaper headquarters about anything and everything: the paper came too late; inserts and flyers weren't folded properly; on rainy days the paper was tied in a *knotted* plastic bag as opposed to a *twist tie*; the paper tube showed cracks and needed replacing; and, my favorite, Mike twirled in circles in front of her house to taunt her, a claim Mike and I respectfully refuted. Most egregious, she refused to pay. The transaction was normally executed by leaving the required cash in an envelope for the paper carrier to collect. Ruth G. had not paid in three weeks, so we simply stopped delivering to her. She complained to headquarters, and Mike was told to deliver her paper. Instead, we stuck a note in her paper tube saying the paper would come once payment was received. Again, she complained, and headquarters insisted we leave Ruth G. her paper. She must have had a picture of Mike's boss with a goat. It had been almost a week of passing her house without delivering when we finally rolled to a stop at her paper tube. Standing triumphant on the front porch with her hands on her hips was the Royal Bitch Ruth G., gloating like a sow who got the last ear of corn. The joke was on her. Mike was in the back seat with a rope. One end was tied to the Jeep's rollbar; the other we'd formed into a lasso. Mike dropped the lasso over the paper delivery tube, and I accelerated, wrenching the tube, post and all, out of the dirt and dragging it down the street bouncing behind us. I did not glance back at Ruth G., but Mike said she had her hand to her mouth. Choking on that ear of corn, I suppose. Mike told headquarters they could keep both the route and Ruth. To our astonishment, they relinquished their position on Mike's earlier demand to drop her as a customer and offered him a transfer to another, more lucrative route. Apparently, newspaper carriers were in short supply and more valuable than any one customer, especially one as bad as Ruth G. Good to know the newspaper had our backs. We learned later from the carrier who replaced us that Ruth was thenceforth a model citizen, never late on payment and even adding a tip, probably the first in her life.

MORAL: Sometimes your company gets involved with people who conflict with its goals. Contain the situation quickly. Then deal with it decisively.

CHAPTER 3

Growing Pains

THERE IS A NATURAL TENDENCY FOR BUSINESS OWNERS TO include growth as one of their key objectives. Growth means the expansion of operations, bigger opportunities, and increased income and industry presence. It also means a strain on cash flow and human resources and the risk of taking on opportunities that the business is not quite mature enough to undertake. Micro-Ant had its share of the latter, and in retrospect the difficulties we fell into could have been easily solved or avoided altogether. If expansion is on your agenda, then your company must have good sustainability and a scalability that is well thought out and easy to follow. Flying by the seat of your pants only gets you so far, and where it does get you usually takes twice as long compared to following a good scalability plan. Despite your very best intentions, there is still that temptation to let faith be your guide even when it comes to making decisions big and small. In this chapter, I describe a transaction we at Micro-Ant entered into with an individual that turned out to be fallacious—both the individual and the transaction. In retrospect, it could not have been otherwise because false dealings require someone false to be involved, and getting through it requires moving forward with a plan that is carefully crafted on integrity—and not on faith.

By 2005, we'd made substantial progress toward being a sustainable business. We were fifteen employees strong and were leasing warehouse and office space to house our operations, which included ongoing light manufacturing. However, our profit-to-sales ratio remained low. After tallying all expenses, our net profits were positive but proportionately low compared to our total revenue. Although we were barely making any net profit, it was fine with me so long as we were financially sustainable and able to keep our staff gainfully employed. Even so, breaking even starts to get old over time, and it was clear we lacked sufficient scalability and needed someone on the team with a solid background in business expansion to put us on that track. But how do you go about persuading a professional business executive of that caliber to join a fledgling company with little to offer by way of compensation? We got lucky when an unscrupulous grandee disguised as a reputable businessperson contacted our company with a proposition that, if fully executed, would likely have put us out of operation.

His name was Little Jimmy. Little Jimmy wanted us to develop and manufacture a mobile satellite tracking antenna that was in demand with law enforcement agencies operating in remote locations where communications were limited, such as along border patrols. This much was accurate, and we undertook the development effort. Once the product was developed, field tested, and type-approved to operate on the satellite network, the discussion turned toward volume production. The lion's share of the effort thus far had been bankrolled by Micro-Ant, and we were eager to recoup this. Settling on a unit price and delivery schedule, Little Jimmy placed a purchase order worth $2.5M. Two point five MILLION dollars! This was a fortune to us, more than we'd made in the previous two years combined. We celebrated the momentous occasion by taking the entire company out to dinner.

There was only one small catch: Little Jimmy had no money and no credit. None. The limo he would show up in was a façade. Stories of NASCAR sponsorship and big-game fishing aboard fancy yachts? A sham. His favorite restaurant? Waffle House. It was a monumental lack of sensibility on my part to not vet the financial wherewithal of this customer. This dreadful lesson taught me to *know your customer*! Unfortunately, this revelation came after we had in process over $100K of custom vendor parts that could not be canceled or returned. Little Jimmy's plan, as he later told me, was to pay us out of the proceeds from the sales he made to his customers. Okay, let's think about that. We were on NET thirty-day terms with our vendors. He was on NET thirty-day terms with his customers, with a ninety-day production lag factored in between invoices. The net result was we'd go broke. In other words, in addition to the sizable development costs we had incurred, we now owed an additional $100K in semi-finished goods that we had no prospect of selling. Things looked desperate from our point of view.

* * *

LIFE LESSON: There was ample weaponry on hand to entertain us boys, including a pair of steel swords and even an old war rifle equipped with a bayonet. I have a permanent scar running down the left side of my chin delivered by Dick during a sword fight where I was Zorro and Dick the scurvy bastard who was just plain bigger and stronger. There was also a hunting bow-and-arrow set in Hank's closet, but we were never allowed to *shoot* it. I emphasize the word "shoot" because even a child can tell you stabbing is not shooting, therefore not off the table. On the day before Thanksgiving, we told Mike that Ma needed a turkey and that we had to bag her one. The joke on Mike was that the turkey was really Dick in disguise making turkey noises. It was a twist on hide-and-seek, and Mike was given occasional clues as to the whereabouts of the turkey by Dick's gobbling. I added my own enrichment to the hunt by equipping Mike with one of the razor-tipped arrows from the aforementioned bow-and-arrow set. Upon discovering the turkey, Mike secured capture by burying the arrow point in its foot, causing blood and an unturkey-like reaction. The finale played out in a short but heated debate. Dick, Mike, and I forever held opposing perspectives of the event, but in hindsight, Mike's is decidedly most accurate. He was lured in under false pretenses, equipped for a particular result, and merely executed the plan as instructed. I fully admitted to the equipping part but not to the execution. Thank God Mike did not go in for a head kill. If there was any blame to be had in this instance, it was upon Dick, who suggested the plan in the first place but set no ground rules.

MORAL: Beware of the Trojan Horse (or Turkey) posing as an opportunity. Common sense and character assessment will help determine if the people you are negotiating with have the wherewithal to hold up their end of the bargain.

* * *

TO OVERCOME THE ENORMOUS FINANCIAL deficit we found ourselves in, Greg and I cut our already meager salaries in half and began working furiously day and night to pull in billing against standing consulting contracts meant to span over a year or more. We knocked them out in weeks, enough to keep payroll afloat for the time being and keep vendors at bay. We went to Little Jimmy and told him there would be no product unless he could come up with some funding to get us through this crisis. To his credit, he did try to find investors willing to buy a stake in this "opportunity." Little Jimmy happened to know somebody who knew our eventual CEO and partner, Jim. I can only imagine the reaction of Jim, a seasoned businessman, when he was approached by these characters. Jim happened to be spending the summer on Cape Cod, not far from where I lived at the time, and invited me to visit and discuss the Little Jimmy fiasco. It was an interview really; he was trying to understand what sort of idiot would get caught up in such an asinine transaction. Whether he felt sorry or intrigued I'm not sure, but he agreed to generate a recovery plan to make Micro-Ant whole and put the burden on Little Jimmy & Son Enterprises, where it properly belonged. In the scheme of things, that toxic business deal was of little consequence, but the meeting it led to with Jim turned out to be everything. Jim in time became our CEO and a stakeholder in the company. He would go on to oversee all business development and was largely responsible for our transformation into a world-class operation.

Jim initiated several changes that put us on the fast track to increased profits. He taught us to stop giving away our intellectual property, or IP. In his view, customers were sponsoring development *services* and were not entitled to IP ownership or rights. What they were funding was the *adaptation* of our IP to their application. They were welcome to use it but in no other way independently exploit it. This was a game changer for us. Companies could no longer (legally) take our IP and manufacture or modify it for any purpose, as had been typical up to that point. Jim rewrote our contracts to reflect this stipulation, and henceforth we retained ownership of everything we developed—on paper at least.

The first time we executed this new strategy was during a meeting at the engineering offices of Sirius Satellite Radio, located near Princeton, New Jersey. We had completed twelve development jobs for Sirius up to that point, including several consumer products that were produced in the millions, netting them many millions of dollars in profit on antenna sales alone. Our compensation for this work was equal to our expenses. In other words, we were just trading dollars, with no real net profit to show for it. The Sirius engineering team were a great group of individuals, and we enjoyed every minute of working for them—but it wasn't exactly a financial bonanza for us. Prior to this meeting, Jim instructed me to tell them that we wanted a one-dollar license fee for each headset they produced that incorporated an antenna design we had previously developed. I stumbled through my proposal, clearly nervous at the boldness of it but determined to see it through, and in the end they acquiesced. Sirius manufactured 350,000 of these headsets and, honoring our agreement, paid us in full. For us, it was like having access to a money machine, and it illustrated how, like the notorious banana stand, the money is in the IP. We never gave it away again.

Jim also focused on the recurring product sales of our business with an objective of making them considerably more profitable. This he did by pricing our products at market value rather than cost-plus. Market value is based on the IP content of the product that enables the customer to achieve their business plan, whereas cost-plus simply marks up the materials, labor, and overhead costs to manufacture the product by some percentage. The cost-plus model is typical of commodity products that compete on price and should never be applied to custom products possessing genuine IP. We've had many customers big and small tell us that it was their policy to own any intellectual property that they sponsored and that it was a condition of doing business with them. We say, "Great, then go buy it from the other guy." Not a single customer—let me repeat, *not a single customer*—has ever refused business with us based on our requirement of owning all the IP we develop, despite their "set in stone" policies. These are the "Who's Who" of business too, and they all agree to it in the end. If you should ever find yourself in a situation where a customer insists on owning your intellectual property on the basis that they funded its development, tell them, "No, you didn't. You funded the *adaptation* of our intellectual property to your application. We were carrying this IP in our brains long before we met you." The bottom line is: keep your IP. If you invented it, you should own it.

***

LIFE LESSON: My parents had gone out for the evening, leaving Hank and Bill to watch over Dick and me. Mike wasn't born yet. To make the night a memorable one, Hank and Bill devised a contest you will likely never see on TV. The rules of the game were quite simple: Hank and Bill would flush some item down the toilet, and Dick and I took turns snaking our arms in and up the flush pipe to retrieve it. I went first and, reaching up to my elbow, got a NICKEL! Dick went next and got the MONOPOLY THIMBLE! What a game! A prize on every turn! Over time the prizes got less and less exciting, but we were having fun. Then it was Dick's turn. At first, he could feel no object, so he kept going deeper and deeper, his face pressed against the opened black pearl toilet seat. Finally, he got hold of something and predicted, incorrectly, that it was a Twinkie. With all the care of a skilled surgeon performing a lobotomy, Dick gingerly extracted, intact, an enormous log of shit. I was disappointed, knowing it would be impossible to top that, which made

Dick the winner. Apparently, my brothers all agreed because the game ended. Hank applied a massive dose of talc powder to Dick's arm to remedy the foul odor. I think the "Twinkie" was a surprise even to them. At the end of it all, Bill tried to take back the nickel. The gall! It was a Buffalo nickel, which was no longer being minted and was going out of circulation. Hank and Bill had a great laugh and got their nickel's worth at our expense, further supporting my claim that I earned it so was not giving it up.

MORAL: If it's your IP, don't undervalue it and certainly don't give it away. It's an asset of your business that, in time, will become critical to scalability.

* * *

AS THE MANUFACTURING ARM OF the company flourished, we knew we needed a bigger facility and extended our search area for a new home base as far as Florida, where we eventually relocated the entire company. Over time we expanded the operation to include a machine shop because it was difficult to find local shops willing and able to meet our stringent demands. As the company grew, our thoughts turned toward making it a sustainable business that would operate without the constant attention of us partners, who also held key positions within the organization. In essence, we needed to find our successors, the next generation of managers and overseers who would be responsible for the visionary strategies and day-to-day operations. To address this, we developed a forward-looking Org chart and hired a president to manage it.

As your business expands, you will no doubt experience your own set of growing pains. It comes with owning a business, and even the best-intentioned planning cannot inoculate you against all pitfalls. My advice is to compartmentalize these adverse situations as you see them unfold and assign a task force to deal with them. This will help isolate the incident from the rest of the company and reduce the scope for those tasked to deal with it. It may well be that you *are* the task force, but no matter. Resolution must begin somewhere. Be sure to give the task force clear direction on the objective and the strategy you have in mind, and see that it is followed precisely. You should also appoint a leader who is ultimately responsible for accomplishing the task. The last thing you want is *decision by committee*, which is the worst possible strategy for solving any problem and dilutes all sense of responsibility. As president of Micro-Ant, I had to deal with all sorts of issues both inside and outside the company as we grew in both size and revenue. Not only did the operation scale as we grew, so did the magnitude of the issues we dealt with. It's the external issues that tend to cause the most pain, like dealing with partners whom you have little control over and ending up in an awkward spot. One day this will become one of your Lessons Learned. In business it's generally true that what does not bankrupt you makes you stronger.

CHAPTER 4

Cultivating Culture

IT IS FAIR TO SAY CULTURE PLAYS A ROLE IN *EVERY* ASPECT of any business, so the successful company is one that nurtures its culture effectively to the benefit of all. But what exactly is culture, and what metrics can be applied to quantify it? Expressed in the simplest terms, culture is the collective attitude of the employees toward the company they work for. All the nuances associated with it are anything but simple because attitude is influenced by countless factors and is manifested in everything we do. It is the atmosphere in which all breathe. It is the life blood of the organization. It is the key element that transforms a *business* into a *company*. Employees want to know first and foremost that the company cares about them. How is this done? By caring about them. In fact, to succeed at anything, first you must care. Otherwise, you've already stacked the odds of succeeding against your favor. Bonuses, gifts, and the like provide short-lived effects but are a meager substitute for genuine consideration. Anyone can figure out quickly whether someone genuinely cares about them or whether they are simply *employed*. Recall my experience with Pradeep, who made it clear his primary interest was the corporate bottom line and that any consideration concerning me, the employees, and the industry we worked in for that matter, was only in how he could exploit it for profit. Despite being a dedicated, faithful employee for over a decade with aspirations of spending my entire career at Seavey Engineering, that single toxic encounter was a tipping point setting me in an entirely new direction, and I never looked back.

Toxicity is defined by the size of the dose, meaning all things are poison if administered in doses too large to process. If an employee who will not submit to authority is an ailment, then a leader unable to lead is a terminal condition. A good leader who is a poor manager or a good manager who is a poor leader will create a condition within the body culture that is difficult to treat. Leadership skills and management skills are not the same any more than being visionary is the same as being detail oriented. Both are valuable aspects of any business but serve distinctly different purposes. To be successful, organizations require a balance of both, with one complementing the other. Each has its proper place and should be dosed carefully in accordance with the needs of the company and its effect upon the culture. The effective leader strategizes the objective while the effective manager implements the plan. The leader and the manager can be one and the same person, but to succeed, the distinction between strategy and tactics must be recognized. Understanding this is critical to effective management. Not understanding this will lead to ineffective management and conflict.

Conflicting management has a 100 percent success rate at creating conflict. Employees will make up their own process without a clear understanding of what process they should follow to execute their tasks. It's a survival mechanism where, in the absence of good management and a clear plan, everyone will fill in the gaps as they see fit, managing themselves in a way that works for them but not necessarily in concert with the rest of the company. This is termed *operating in a silo*. A silo, as anyone who has visited a farm can tell you, is a storage tower used to hold grain, keeping it isolated from the wide-open field from which it was recently harvested. In the context of the business idiom, the grain is replaced by data that has been harvested and kept isolated and inaccessible from the rest of the company. Instead of using a central database such as a Materials Resource Planning (MRP) system that can be shared company-wide, the silo operator creates personalized spread-sheets to track and store information, accessible only by them. This leads to *departments* becoming *compartments*, creating virtual boundaries that block the flow of vital information. When people decide for themselves how they should be doing their own jobs, it's only a matter of time before they decide on how others should be doing *theirs*. Once the situation escalates to this level, communication across the company breaks down, and established processes are ignored. Management becomes increasingly ineffective until it is all but impotent. Poorly managed employees will continue employing additional mechanisms toward self-preservation, compartmentalizing themselves further. Any semblance of being a team evaporates. When you no longer have a team, you no longer have a company. The cascade of effects that follow can bring a company to stagnation. The key is to recognize the signs and take corrective action to circumvent the disorder before paralysis sets in.

The disposition of a culture is built upon many things, in particular emotional reactions to events taking place within the organization that are difficult to rationalize. The temper of any employee's mood depends on how they view company leadership because culture and leadership are tightly coupled. It might be possible that an unfavorable culture can exist despite good leadership, but it's unlikely that the converse would occur. Human nature is too powerful. We are emotional creatures who demand good leadership and well-structured discipline. This is something I can relate to personally. Some highly educated people in my field have criticized me for not being scientific or for being undisciplined in my approach to solving problems despite a successful track record of antenna innovation spanning three decades. If we were to substitute the word "criticized" with "credited," then we'd have an accord. It is true; my creative, artistic side allows me to see the solution almost instantaneously while my scientific counterpart extracts this information bit by bit over a much longer period until the solution materializes. This has been key to my success. With art we *create*; with science we *explain*. Art is the creative expression of our emotions, so taking that away, we are reduced to scientists, sterile in our approach to problem-solving. Cultures are built upon expressions of emotion, so it takes a disciplined yet creative approach to manage them. But how do we go about it?

* * *

LIFE LESSON: When I was around four years old, my parents went out for the evening, leaving Hank and Bill to watch over Dick and me. All four of us shared the same bedroom, which featured two double-decker bunkbeds set up on opposite walls. Dick and I had the top bunks because we weighed much less than Hank and

Bill so were less likely to initiate a collapse of the top bed upon the lower occupant, which was known to happen from time to time. Hank ordered Dick and me off to bed, so we each retired to our respective upper bunks. Shortly after, Bill came in screaming, followed by Hank wielding a razor knife. Bill held in his hand an eyeball, recently cut from its socket by Hank. Where his eye should have been was instead a gaping hole dripping of blood and hanging tissue. I joined in with Bill screaming, which was the purpose of their ruse. Dick may have been screaming too; I was too consumed by my own fear to take notice. Of course, the "eyeball" in Bill's hand was actually an unshelled hard-boiled egg, the "blood" was ketchup, and the hanging "tissue" was peanut butter. Looking back as an adult, it's laughable to think we would have fallen for such an obvious prank, but at the time and given the evidence in/at hand, it took no convincing that Hank had indeed cut out Bill's eye with a razor knife and that Bill stood for it. Had I been older than four, I would have known how unlikely it was that the first impulse of someone who just had their eye gouged out would be to go show his little brothers instead of calling an ambulance or at least putting a bandage on the damn thing.

* * *

IT TAKES GOOD MANAGEMENT TO promote a good culture. Maybe I've said this already, and if so, I'm saying it again. Effective management is not simply about getting your employees to follow processes or carry out instructions, or about managing attitudes and actions. Your approach needs to be one of love and encouragement such that everyone delights in showing themselves in their work. In time, encouragement can lead to inspiration and a mood of being valued and appreciated—appreciated not only by managers and coworkers but by many others, both seen and unseen, who benefit from the love and care expressed in the work. Building "widgets" and being managed by quotas cannot be nearly as rewarding as being part of a unified team. On the other hand, understanding the application of products we create and relating to those who use them can be quite rewarding because an identifiable purpose is being served.

Imagine you own a bakery, and someone comes in to buy a delicious, freshly baked apple pie. Upon completing the transaction, you box and bag the pie and hand it to the customer with a big smile and the customary "Thank you for your business." As the customer exits the shop, they drop the pie into the garbage barrel and continue along their way. How does this make you feel? Would you not care, understanding that this odd customer, having paid for the pie and taken ownership, was free to dispose of it as they wished? Or are you disappointed that the pie will not be enjoyed or, perhaps more importantly, that your effort in crafting the pie will go unappreciated and that the part of you that was a key ingredient now resides alongside the trashed pie in the garbage can? I can personally relate to the trashed pie metaphor because in the early days of Micro-Ant, we saw many pies go into the trash, sometimes by the bakers themselves but more often by customers who lost interest, misjudged the market opportunity, took the recipe for themselves, or simply disappeared without a trace. This happens less and less these days as we do a better job scrutinizing our potential customers and their path to market and insist they have some skin in the game. But I'll tell you, it sucks to see some novel technology or well-thought-out design languish on a shelf. Even the most seasoned professional is susceptible to the disappointment such an outcome brings; it stomps on enthusiasm and has a terrible impact on culture. Every employee is a stakeholder in the company, so there is a part of everyone in each product we design, build, and sell. Keep the human factor alive in what you do; celebrate it with your employees.

The point is that it is unrealistic to think that you can force or purchase a positive attitude because it is influenced by factors money can't buy. A better approach is to be a constructive influence, lead honestly and with integrity, and encourage an atmosphere that nurtures a positive-minded culture. Epidemiology teaches us that a virus, or even an idea for that matter, introduced and modestly sustained will typically infect up to 90 percent of a population, with 70 percent exhibiting a detectable reaction. Applying this model to a company workforce, "vaccinating" your team with a positive attitude and sustaining it will in time yield a positive reaction upon the majority. The key is to foster constructive actions that build a stronger workforce culture while rejecting those that destroy it. Do not let people's emotions, especially your own, stand in the way, but recognize that they exist and play a large role in the decisions we make. Be rational and on hand to explain issues affecting your team before they cause confusion or consternation. A happy person tends to make positive decisions.

Our company offers several perks to employees such as free lunches on Wednesdays, costume parties, and an annual Christmas feast with games, prizes, and bonuses given out. The Wednesday lunch came about when a long-time employee was leaving the company and we threw them a farewell party. It was such a success that we decided to hold these catered lunches *every* Wednesday, mixing up the fare by ordering from select local restaurants. Small gestures like this tend to go a long way toward promoting morale. Speaking of gestures, I like to personally greet some of the engineers each morning by giving them the middle finger. I also silently mouth the meaning of that finger—you know, for reinforcement. By the smiles on their faces, it appears to be every bit a morale booster equal to free coffee and donuts but without the pesky type 2 diabetes. Not a single complaint to HR either, that I've heard of anyway.

We view culture for the true, living entity that it is and consider it in nearly every decision we make. Our Chief Operating Officer, or COO, makes regular rounds to each department and spends time with the employees, asking whether they need anything and if there is anything he can do to help. His job, primarily, is to put in place all elements needed for us to succeed, including an atmosphere that promotes a positive attitude and transparency. This is also an opportunity to communicate our value and appreciation of and to the team, and this practice continues. In a small business, the company and the managers are viewed as one and the same, so culture is essentially the collective attitude of the employees toward their *managers and employers*. Swiftly address and correct issues that arise in a negative perception. Never let them fester.

* * *

LIFE LESSON: Mike's early interest in being a farmer led to a livestock community consisting of three ducks and two chickens. Their names were Green Duck, White Duck, Brown Duck, Woodstock, and The Other Chicken. Brown Duck was by far Mike's favorite because it was the offspring of Green Duck and White Duck, who produced but one egg to hatch into a living duckling, which Mike cared for intently. Usually, the flock ranged freely about the yard foraging in the grass, but in winter they were kept together in the barn and fed cracked corn from a sack. One freezing morning after Mike left for school, I went out to feed them, and discovered Brown Duck, stone-cold dead. Close examination revealed a small wound in the poor duck's head, which I deduced was a lethal peck administered by one of the two chickens. I told Dick, and we both felt pretty bad, knowing this was Mike's favorite. We could not leave Brown Duck lying there, and since the ground was too frozen for a burial, we put it in the woodstove for cremation. The fire being hot, the duck exploded, probably because of gasses trapped in the body. The sound was alarming, and the smell of burnt feathers saturated the entire house. It was like a Stephen King horror movie. I was not there when Mike came home, so Dick broke the news to him.

When I followed up with Mike to share my condolences, he seemed more angry than sad, which I thought to be an objection to our method of interment. Many, many years later, at the wedding of Mike's son, James, somehow the story of the ducks came up, and I remarked that most likely one of the chickens killed it. Mike said, "What are you talking about?! Dick said you were angry and whipped a wrench that hit its head, killing it instantly." *"I what!? I did no such thing!"* We turned to Dick, who was also sitting at the table. He burst out laughing, saying, "I don't think that's what I said." It wasn't convincing enough for Mike or me. What the hell? For thirty years Mike carried in his head that I killed his favorite pet, with a wrench, for the hell of it?? This served to substantiate in me the subtle but perceptible change in our relationship I imagined began on that day. Not sure if or how Mike's attitude toward me was affected by this misunderstanding, but it sure would have been nice to have dealt with it properly at the time.

MORAL: Address and correct issues before they become false dogma. Where possible address them on the spot and do so with honesty and compassion.

* * *

HOW WE VIEW AND USE technology as a company bears brief mention because it plays such a key role in how we operate. The setting has become commonplace for businesses to employ a wide range of technologies throughout their organizations. Like most companies, we use software for the purpose of data simulation, collection, and processing, and to control various machinery and instrumentation. Product development starts in the engineering department, where the product concept is defined as a numerical model using CAD software, then simulated and optimized to meet customer requirements. The product of this effort is transferred via electronic file for mechanical configuration, which serves both to document the product design and provide the milling instructions to the Computer Numerical Control (CNC) machines in our fabrication shop. The CNC-milled components are inspected via Coordinate Measuring Machine (CMM) and then go on to production, where they are assembled into a product using a combination of manual, machine-assisted, and automated operations. Every operation within the product workflow process employs some level of technology to accomplish its successful completion.

In our case, one thing technology *does not* do is replace people. Our purpose in using technology is to reduce human error and to improve product quality and reliability. Any increase in human efficiency translates into an increase in production capacity, not a reduction in workforce. Automation, too, is used to augment a particular operation but still requires a worker to supervise it. The point is that we do not replace employees with machines. It is our view that the company has a responsibility to the community in which it resides to provide meaningful employment to its residents. A covenant exists between community and corporation in which each brings value to the other, and together they share in the prosperity. The decisions we make as a company always consider our employees and our community. Properly employed, technology is simply an idea set in motion to facilitate human productivity. The intelligent business runs the technology; the technology does not run the business.

Perhaps the most important takeaway from this chapter is the importance of caring, truly caring, about the people you work with. This is not typically a difficult thing, but getting through to people who work in an environment sterile of self-expression and job satisfaction can be *very* difficult. I often hear employees refer to their workmates as family, which is a wonderful sentiment. But how often do you hear families compliment their siblings by calling them workmates? As much as I enjoyed growing up in my family, I would not wish that culture upon my employees. The key to showing that you care is to listen—and listen often. Sometimes people want to talk, sometimes they need to vent, and sometimes they want resolution. Sometimes they simply want to know what the hell is going on. Offer an open, sympathetic ear, and where possible pass on their concerns to the person who can offer resolution. A lot of businesses "shield" employees from the hard facts of business life; I'm not a big proponent of this. I believe in being transparent in all things that directly affect that individual's well-being and permitting them the dignity of dealing with such information maturely and as any adult. It makes for a stronger employee-employer relationship, a wonderful culture, and a better company overall.

CHAPTER 5

(In)effective Leadership

THE TRAITS THAT MAKE SOMEONE A GOOD LEADER HAVE been written about and debated for years upon years. I like to put things as simply as possible so I can understand and explain them. My simplified definition of a leader is a person others are willing to follow. They are generally willing to follow their leader for three reasons: (1) they believe the leader is acting in their best interests; (2) the leader has a noble objective to pursue; (3) the leader has a plan to accomplish the objective that all can understand and follow. Being paid to follow a person might give the illusion of leadership, but it is not true leadership. I spent so much time searching out various leaders for Micro-Ant it escaped me that the best-suited leader for the company turned out to be far closer than I ever expected. It turned out to be me. This was somewhat of a surprise to me at the time, but now looking back it seems so obvious. What I lacked then was the benefit of observing an ineffective leader and the disruption it caused to the organization. It was a Lesson Learned, on the job so to speak, that challenged me to discover my suppressed traits of leadership and put them to good use.

At one time or another, I have held every position within the company. That's not hard to do, especially if you are the only employee. As the company grows, you must be willing to recognize the point where it has outgrown your ability to manage certain things and assign these responsibilities to those more experienced and capable than you. The decision to make Jim CEO was a no-brainer. That he was willing to accept the position was the surprising part. At the time, he was living in blissful retirement, content with his self-imposed routine of pro bono work, legal- and business-related. His adventurous spirit overcame his rational thinking, prompting him to take hold of the reins of our emerging, high-tech business. He saw something in us and chose to pursue it, to our great fortune. Jim focused on business development and corporate strategy while Greg and I immersed ourselves in engineering duties, and together we searched for someone to oversee the operation and execute our strategic vision. We'd had a president once before, briefly, but simply weren't ready at the time to support that kind of overhead. But now, with nearly seventy employees and on a steady growth trajectory, we were ripe for it, all other key positions having been defined, filled, and ready for the new leadership. This being an important position, it was vital to choose wisely who filled it. We were fortunate to find and hire a seasoned professional named Scott, who boasted extensive leadership experience at both large-scale and startup high-tech companies.

A degreed engineer with a background in antenna technology and experience managing large engineering teams, Scott was the perfect fit for president. We empowered him with all the authority and resources necessary to succeed and set him loose. Our mandate to him was clear—"grow the company"—and he took it quite seriously and spent much time with Jim studying the principles required to navigate us into the future. Upon his own investigation of the company and its situation, Scott correctly recognized that we performed poorly regarding on-time delivery, and this became his central focus as he managed the various departments and resources of the firm. The stratagem was simple—meet our delivery commitments *on time*, and it will lead to prosperity, i.e., the company will grow. It could be summed up as follows:

- *The objective: grow the business*

- *The strategy: deliver on time*

- *The plan: bully everyone into succeeding*

Excluding the bullying part, in any other context this seems a sound philosophy, cogent and even clever. Yet the method of its implementation led to consequences both deleterious and perplexing.

Scott is quite intelligent and unquestionably competent as a manager and a technical director, but somehow there was some missing element that prevented him from being viewed as a good leader, an individual whom others were willing to follow. His objective was certainly one that we all could get behind, but his plan for getting us all there was not well laid out. As such, no one felt that he had our best interests in mind. Clearly, he favored the customer over those who were tasked to do the actual work of manufacturing and shipping products. Scott's commitment to the customers put his reputation on the line, and it was apparent that this was what drove him as much, if not more, than anything else. It is now clear exactly why the on-time-delivery strategy did not work, although at the time it was not so obvious. Within Micro-Ant, we would have universally agreed that Scott's leadership style was aggressive and prone to micromanagement, but it was not until the dust settled following his departure that the term *bully* was passed around. In retrospect, that was the heart of the problem and the reason we gained no ground on our growth objective but instead actually began slipping backward. This sort of leadership might look good in certain situations, but as a long-term approach it only breeds resentment.

* * *

LIFE LESSON: Hank and Bill took me fishing when I was about five. It was a rare thing to include me in anything that did not involve being staked down and whipped with a holly branch. I don't recall being allowed to fish, but just being along was glorious. On the way back home, they realized that some item or other was forgotten at the fishing hole and they needed to go back to get it. They left me to watch the eight or so fish they had caught. Seated as I was next to an open drainpipe that disappeared into darkness as it bored downward, they added the following instruction:

"Do not throw the fish down that drainpipe, or we will beat the hell out of you."

From their perspective it was a sound stratagem, clearly spelling out both the directive and the consequence, thereby ensuring fish for dinner. But there were two flaws in their proposal:

1. I had no intention of throwing the fish down the drainpipe until they put the idea in my head.

2. Offering consequence without reward is not much of an incentive.

The second they left I threw the fish down the drainpipe. The way I saw it, I was going to get beaten anyway. If not then, at some later point in time for some unspecified transgression. So may as well get something in return for it now. I was even convinced that's what they wanted me to do, or else why bother mentioning it in the first place? The story ends as you may imagine, with my brothers executing upon me their promised reward, adding to this a token bonus at my refusal to climb down the pipe to retrieve the fish.

MORAL: Threats are not incentives and tend to produce undesirable results. Lead with the carrot, not the stick.

* * *

WHAT IS THE CONNECTION BETWEEN tossing fish down a drainpipe and the on-time-delivery ploy? Both were executed by threatening consequences instead of providing an incentive. For Hank and Bill, the incentive was keeping the fish. For our president, the incentive was upholding his reputation, having personally given his word to customers that he would unfailingly meet their delivery needs. But what about the rest of the company? If deliveries were not met on time, it was *our* fault. We failed. And if the delivery *was* made on time? We avoided the blame for the time being and were temporarily spared the sense of being marked a failure. That was hardly an incentive. One may argue that delivering on time is a wholly rational precept, and the reward comes from invoicing earlier, satisfying the customer, and all that company gung-ho speak. But these things are generally invisible to the employees who perform the work so are meaningless incentives at best. In addition, the outcome may well be completely out of their control in the first place. After two years of executing this strategy, there was no doubt that we made considerable improvement meeting our on-time deliveries. Success! But no, morale within the company dropped precipitously, and there was a growing number of product returns, in nearly all cases related to poor workmanship.

It became commonplace to expect product failures during the assembly process and product returns, so Quality Assurance (QA) built a cage, a jail in which to store these culprits, apparently forever. These poor products sat on death row with no action taken because, quite frankly, QA at the time had no process for resolving the problem, so in the cage they went. But no one could argue that we were doing a much better job shipping on time. We were cutting corners in our manufacturing process to save time, only to pay ninefold later. QA was overwhelmed trying to keep things in order and was often bypassed so product flow could continue uninterrupted. As a rule, we blamed QA for the delays and for the return of defective products. How could they let this happen!? It was an intractable situation.

We did a prodigious job getting the on-time delivery message through the company but failed to explain how it was to be accomplished. Meeting followed by meeting followed by meeting was held to reinforce *what* but never *how*. Each day started with a two-hour meeting attended by representatives from every department. To this day, the objective of these is still lost on me. Now, I'm not opposed to meetings, but they should be spontaneous rather than scheduled. In my view, meetings are too often used as compensation for ineffective management. In most cases, a little footwork can accomplish the same thing and without wasting a lot of people's time, especially if the flow of information is one-way. The stated purpose of the "Morning Meetings" did not align with their outcome, and they became viewed as opportunities for Scott to gather ammunition to be used against us later when his shifting expectations were not met. Each meeting was like a gut punch to employee morale. A bully session. No one feels good about shipping defective products, but it was better than being a target for blame. But blame was coming either way. There was no winning. It could be argued that many factors might just as well have contributed to the ultimate problem, but I have since spent considerable time in the trenches listening and learning things that can only be acquired in trenches, and I stand by my assertion that the fundamental issues were the lack of an organized plan and a leader who lacked empathy for his employees. We successfully unified ourselves behind a central strategy but failed to establish the tactics necessary to support it. We were acting almost entirely on the principle that if the intent was good, the result should be too.

* * *

LIFE LESSON: Who doesn't remember the game *Scatter!*? In our version, we would stand in a circle with Hank in the middle. He would take his hunting bow and shoot a broadhead arrow straight up into the air, yelling, "Scatter!" We would all run and take shelter in different locations to avoid the descending arrow—and death. You won if the arrow landed closest to your sheltering spot. Dick once hid beneath our garden tractor, and the arrow struck between its two front tires, inches from his foot, making him winner for life. Hank and Bill took delight in devising games like this to entertain us boys, and there was always an element of risk involved in each. They constructed a variety of amusements around the house for our recreation. Dick and I were the only customers to grace the "park," and reluctant ones at that. The amusements included the Roller Coaster, which delivered more rolling than coasting; the Tornado, consisting of a wooden box suspended from a high tree branch by a cable, the rider being spun mercilessly until sobbing like a second-grade schoolgirl; Airplane Glide, which was a wheelbarrow outfitted with a wooden plank for wings, piloted by one of my brothers who simulated turbulence to enhance the experience; and the Parachute Jump, aka Leap of Faith, which involved jumping from the barn roof clutching an optional oversized beach umbrella. Dick preferred the Leap of Faith sans umbrella, as if there were any choice in it. In a grand display of faith, he leapt thirteen times in a row from the barn roof, which caused him to limp for several months until my mother took notice that it was getting worse and took Dick to the hospital. An X-ray of the leg uncovered not only a fractured femur head but also a small tumor on the end closest to the knee. To make matters worse, Dick had hit a growth spurt, and his good leg had outgrown the affected one. It took a series of operations on *both* legs to rectify the problem, and to this day Dick carries a matching set of massive scars but an unmatched set of legs, which differ in length by an inch or so. If this was the outcome that Dick's faith was to protect him against, his gave out somewhere around the tenth leap.

MORAL: In business, you cannot operate solely on faith or intent. A strategy needs a good plan to succeed.

* * *

OVER TIME, OUR ONCE-ESTEEMED PRESIDENT became ineffective as a leader and generally viewed within the organization as disingenuous and a *bully*. In all fairness, Scott did not come across this way in a nonprofessional setting, so likely his unpleasant behavior was in response to our loosely structured environment, which to him may have been unfamiliar and uncomfortable. If anything, Scott was an outsider, out of touch with our corporate culture and thus ill-equipped to succeed at instituting any plan that would be, let alone *could* be, followed. This one stratagem—deliver on time—had been executed as though an obsession, serving to undermine his ability to lead or maintain any sense of authority and leaving him bereft of the respect he otherwise deserved.

Not a single department went unscathed. Growth was essentially stagnant over that two-year period, and no one really understood why at the time. Revenue was steady, but profitability dipped. It was both perplexing and frustrating and a time for brutal honesty and reflection. We broke the company or at the very least bruised it. It was like the boiling frog allegory, where you find yourself in an adverse situation that has transpired in degrees too small to notice until the full context of it all is upon you, and by then you're cooked.

At the nadir of this dismal period, Scott retired. The mood within the company and especially amongst the managers upon the departure of this dedicated, earnest, and hardworking leader was...relief. It would be the end of an era, a disappointing period in our corporate history, and a lesson never to be forgotten. It was an electric handshake and a mouthful of dog shit rolled into one. If I were to sum up the major flaw with the on-time delivery plan, it would be that it lacked salability, both in the plan and in the person. Although I did not hire this individual or have the opportunity to interview him, I take full responsibility for the problem that ensued because I knew and understood early on that this person had no salability, lacked sensibility, and therefore could never rally together a team to support his way of thinking.

* * *

FOLLOWING THE ON-TIME DELIVERY FIASCO, the company mood was the lowest I had witnessed since our inception. Even the sentiment during the Little Jimmy episode was a celebration by comparison. To get us back on track, it was important to first understand what each person was feeling and why. It had nothing to do with the incentives we offered. Everyone felt disconnected and that management did not care about them, at least not as much as delivering products on time to customers. When I assumed the role of president, I felt like an outsider myself, out of touch with our culture since I'd spent the past few years in a nonmanagerial role. We had nearly seventy employees, many whose names I didn't even know. If I was to bond with our team, we needed to get to know one another better, and I needed to listen carefully to everything they were willing to share.

To learn everyone's name I had each department make a list of every team member and their two favorite colors. Swordy Moon was engaged and got busy making every employee their own custom-colored duffle bag. The effort burnt into my memory the name of every employee and what two colors they like. Since I already have a color stored in my head for every word, number, song, or person, it was a helpful aid when face recognition alone failed me. It also gave me some quality time with each person and allowed me to pick up something interesting or unique about them.

Another thing we did was start teaching antenna classes at a layperson's level to each department so they could gain an appreciation of what we do as a company. First and foremost, the classes were meant to build shared understanding and camaraderie among the team. Many had heard and even used the jargon associated with antenna technology but did not understand the meaning. We taught employees how to identify our various products and the functions they provided. It was impressive to see people with little or no technical background quickly pick up the terminology and employ it correctly. Lecturing also helped me assess the strengths of those attending the classes and gauge their interest in comprehending concepts outside of their familiarity. The antenna classes were a hit. They were intended to augment the appreciation we held toward our employees, and the payback was bilateral. A noticeable improvement in overall mood, quality of work, and productivity was observed. People started enjoying their jobs again.

Hopefully, you will never have to deal with a situation that causes the mood and optimism of your company culture to do a nosedive, as occurred with Micro-Ant. It may happen, though, that influences unseen and unknown do infiltrate your organization. Such problems often reveal themselves through unhappy, griping employees and unusually high employee turnover. The situation can be especially confounding when the reasons are unclear, even to the very people who are suffering. The first step to fixing the issue is to listen—and listen well, as I did. Even if the reason for the unhappy workforce doesn't become entirely clear, there are still many things that can be done. I gave examples of what worked for Micro-Ant, such as sewing custom bags for the employees, offering open lectures, and providing a full-service cafe with free coffee, snacks, and occasional lunches. These initiatives are meant to bring people together, independent of department or work assignment, into a setting where they can enjoy one another's company and socialize with the managers and company leaders.

I take great pleasure in providing an environment where employees can thrive and express their inner selves. My desire is to help them achieve their full growth potential and empower them to do their very best work. The true value of Micro-Ant, as with any successful operation, is in the unity of the team and dedication to a common purpose. They choose to follow me, and it is my privilege to serve these fine people as their leader. By adopting this philosophy, you will make great strides toward developing a team culture based on mutual respect, appreciation, and trust.

CHAPTER 6

A New Focus on Program Management

PROGRAM MANAGEMENT IS A DISCIPLINE INTENDED TO BRING structure and process to an organization. It can be viewed both as a job responsibility and as a concept. Unlike traditional managers, the program manager (PM) as a *person* does not manage people but rather the processes that people follow, across departmental boundaries and all levels of responsibility. Where a manager of a department has authority over those assigned to them, the PM has no authority over personnel. Program management as a *concept* is responsible for setting priorities and determining the strategies for how the company meets its goals. It is the roadmap that takes a project from cradle to grave. It is also, unfortunately, an important position that many small businesses do not fill. At the very least, the functions of the PM should be instituted in every company interested in scalability. Growing takes planning, careful planning, right down to the nitty gritty details of shaping your products and services, and program management is a key tool for accomplishing growth profitably.

Program management instituted as either a person or a concept will reveal gaps in management and will expose bottlenecks in the workflow process that governs how a company operates. Symptoms of ineffective management include the following:

- Priorities are ignored.

- Processes are not followed.

- The wrong people are assigned to the wrong task.

- Information silos are created.

- Communication breakdowns occur.

Benefits of effective management, facilitated by a competent program management plan, include the following:

- Priorities are clearly communicated.

- Information transfers quickly.

- The right people are assigned to the right task.

- Everyone has a well-defined understanding of what they are responsible for.

In short, people know what's going on and never feel left in the dark.

Q1 of 2020 brought a flurry of business activity the likes of which we had never experienced. Our backlog of quotes was at least double the dollar value in comparison to any other year in our history. We put ourselves in a precarious position by accepting orders with no clear-cut path to meeting deadlines for the volumes requested. Production output continued to fall significantly short of the opportunities in hand. It was like sitting on a powder keg set to go off at any moment. Many things were at play, but we eventually got everything under control once effective program management arrived on the scene. Our road to that end was not a clear one at the time, and I did not even know what program management was. We dealt with threats to the business the best way we knew how, calling on lessons from the past to get us through.

A major threat to our growth plans was machine shop capacity and efficiency. We had enough of the right machines and plenty of staff to oversee their operation, yet our capacity remained at less than twenty-five percent of what should reasonably be expected. No matter what software we purchased or what specialized tools and whiz bang gadgetry we had, we simply could not make the needle move in the right direction. After soliciting the opinions of numerous experts on what steps should be taken, we finally arrived at a conclusion—we had to figure this out for ourselves. We went through a similar situation with our production floor but found the fix in Jeff, an employee we'd promoted from test technician to production supervisor and then ultimately to COO. Although Jeff had little background training in this area, his positive attitude, talent for organizing, and sharp leadership skills produced rapid success. We needed similar intervention in the machine shop if we were to turn things around.

The individual we had assigned to the chief operations position was as wonderful a person as you will ever meet. He was thoughtful, polite, and well-liked, but came from a background where structures were already in place and needed only to be followed as opposed to participating in the problem-solving process that comes with evolving strategies. Consequently, we reassigned James from chief engineer to vice president of operations, or VPO. James's mechanical engineering background and experience in machine shop practices permitted him to effect the positive changes we were looking for. James is process-oriented and an advocate for establishing, documenting, and following procedures to the letter.

After an initial assessment of the shop, we concluded that no consistent process was being followed, and any process that did exist differed from operator to operator, from machine to machine, and finally from job to job. The shop was in disarray, and we were fooling only ourselves to have claimed otherwise. It was not always this way; however, the situation had exacerbated following the on-time delivery era when things like following process and QA oversight were discarded in favor of meeting commitment dates. Once James began redefining machine processes and supervising their execution, it was like seeing an old car engine that had been sitting idle and unattended in a field suddenly fire up and run on all cylinders. Not at full throttle by any means, but on all cylinders. The issues in the shop were not new to us. We had just been pushing them off to address more pressing concerns. If these had been dealt with in earnest and openness, we might have saved ourselves the trouble of reorganizing the machine shop and the considerable pain that came with it.

***

LIFE LESSON: In a time not so long ago, shopping from home meant picking items from a catalog, filling out an order form, sealing the form along with payment in a stamped envelope, and getting it into the hands of the US Postal Service. Then waiting for delivery. The delivery could take weeks, months, or, just as likely, not show up at all. A Mr. Peanut pen I ordered in the third grade showed up after I had graduated to the fourth, and the Invisibility Goggles I ordered either never arrived or, if they did, lived up to their name. There was nobody to complain to; let the buyer beware. If the item *did* show up, it was momentous and the item was regarded as being rare, precious, and irreplaceable. So, when the two oversized scientific balloons that Hank and Bill ordered finally arrived, the family enthusiastically rallied to the occasion, setting up a picnic table outdoors as my mother got busy cooking in the kitchen. All this for two rubber balloons. Hank and Bill set up the Hoover outdoors and configured it to blow rather than suck, and—success!—each balloon slowly but surely expanded into its inflated state. If they warned me once, they warned me ten times to stay the hell away from the balloons, but if either Hank or Bill were to look back with openness and honesty, they would have to take partial responsibility for the occurrence that followed. It would have been far wiser to keep me close by. Instead, the "Stay the Hell Away" perimeter encompassing the balloon action kept getting larger and larger to the point where my contribution to the fun could only be executed through loud shouting and vigorous body movements. Here's what played out. Not being allowed to participate directly in my brothers' grand experiment, I involved myself indirectly by picking up a stick and rotating it above my head, pretending to be a helicopter hovering just beyond the no-fly-zone they'd imposed. Everyone knows helicopters were not as safe then as they are now, and the one I was piloting discharged its rotating blade in the direction of Hank, Bill, and the balloons. Here I screamed, *"Watch out for the HELICOPTER!"* Unfortunately, it went unheeded by the very people who could have benefited from this information most. Let me ask you this. If someone yells, *"Watch out for the HELICOPTER!"* what do you do? Natural reactions would be to duck, put your hands over your head for protection, shield your genitals, something. Who would ignore such a warning? Afterward, Dick said that I yelled, *"Here comes the whirling HELICOPTER!"* That is incorrect and would have implied that I ejected the rotating blade deliberately. Guess what? Not one, but both balloons were instantaneously disintegrated by a throw that could not have been executed more precisely had I practiced for a year. The sight of Hank and Bill frozen, arms supporting two balloons that were no longer there, is forever etched in my brain. As reprisal for the deed, my brothers hung me from a pine tree branch, not by the neck but by my underwear, still worn, the elastic waistband proving to be constructed of much sturdier stuff than the two expired balloons. Note: it was I who taught the lesson, not my brothers, because had they kept me close at hand and not banished me to restricted airspace it might have been weeks before I destroyed their balloons. Shame on them.

> **MORAL:** Confront potential problems openly and honestly before they become actual problems and someone ends up hanging from a tree by their underwear.

* * *

IN HIS ROLE AS CHIEF engineer, James had three main responsibilities: (1) manage the engineering team; (2) ensure that engineering design and documentation processes were maintained at the high standards we set; and (3) program management. Program management properly executed is vital to any organization, especially those that are trying to have a meaningful impact on the world through technological innovation. Technological innovation, or innovation of any kind for that matter, requires a team of creative individuals who are intelligent and care deeply for their field of expertise. It has been my experience that this sort of person also tends to be a bit wacky or at the very least display subtle, albeit obvious, quirks that otherwise hamper productivity if not managed skillfully. I am living proof. It was not enough that I had four brothers growing up; I had to create a fifth: *Smonkeewillow*. Smonkee and I were the closest of buddies, as close as any two non-imaginary people could ever be, and he kept me constant company right up to the day he was shot dead by our mutual arch enemy, *Turkey-Me-Alright*. So it goes.

James's appointment to VPO left voids in engineering that desperately needed filling in order to keep this critical part of our organization on course. To manage the team, we divided it into its three disciplines—Electrical, Mechanical, and Active Radio Frequency—and appointed a lead engineer to oversee each. Oversight of engineering process and documentation was assigned to a new position we created to assist in organizing workflow, the engineering documentation controller (EDC). This left program management open, wide open. Until our new program manager came on board, I could not have articulated the essential duties of this role or foreseen its impact toward making us a world-class engineering team. She taught us that program managers are responsible for delivering a large portfolio of different projects—usually connected in theme, timing, or set of resources. Unlike a project manager, who might be the organizational backbone for one to three projects, a program manager's portfolio is usually beyond the capabilities of any one person to track, push along, etc. Because of this, a program manager's role is as much about creating, maintaining, and evolving the systems and structures that enable projects to run smoothly as it is about chasing down the tasks and details of projects. Some examples of this include the following:

- Implementing technologies that simplify workflow, creating access to information, or otherwise empowering and increasing the productivity of individual contributors

- Creating processes and standards that enable teams to work together smoothly and produce consistently good results

- Matching people to jobs and ensuring that there's clarity on prioritization and allocation of work

- Cultivating the culture of the company within the teams—culture is the "glue" that enables people to work well together and is one of the key things that attracts (or repels) great talent to (or from) an organization

- Coaching team members, especially team leads and managers, and helping them implement structure in their teams

- Synthesizing across projects to understand current and future priorities, challenges, and opportunities at both the individual project and the program level

Having a competent, skilled program manager in place was reminiscent of how my sister, Mary Ann, would take notice of us younger boys and our various doings. Her involvement in our activities was the antithesis of what we came to expect from Hank or Bill and was geared more toward the purpose of our personal development.

* * *

LIFE LESSON: Dick and I spent an inordinate amount of leisure time fishing. The only activity we dedicated more time to was breathing, but fishing remained a close second. You would think two people who focused so much time toward a single activity would have achieved a high level of proficiency, yet that was not the case. The problem was, as Dick once pointed out to me, we simply did not pay attention to details. For instance, the outboard motor would stall or choose not to start, but we lived with it. There was a hole somewhere in the hull that leaked incessantly, but rather than fix it we bailed whenever the boat would no longer get on plane—and so on. Our gear was generally in ill repair and prone to falling apart or breaking. Details. We measured our success by what we didn't lose on each trip as opposed to what fish we caught. The following mishap epitomizes the forces and forsaken details that conspired against our success. Dick and I were chasing bluefish schools in New Bedford Harbor using the flocking birds to navigate us toward the feeding fish. The trick was to get in front of the action at racing speed, throw the motor out of gear, and cast our lures into the frenzy of fish, birds, and bait. Making it trickier was the fact that we could never shut off the engine, lest it not start again. Dick would stand at the tip of the bow, which might seem dangerous to the uninformed reader but was necessary for three reasons: (1) he guided me, the pilot, to the next school of fish, (2) it put him in an ideal position to cast into the fish-feeding melee, and (3) his bodyweight provided the counter ballast essential for getting the boat on plane. This was all going well when, during our next blitz run, I noticed one of the rods left in the stern had come unbaled and the lure was free spooling behind the boat. I lurched aft to grab the rod before it went over, but in so doing, my t-shirt, which had billowed in the wind, draped itself over the motor control lever and shifted us into reverse. I had just enough time to turn forward and see Dick in mid-air, far beyond the bow, executing a perfect spread eagle, still clutching the rod in his outstretched left hand. His momentum carried him an additional twenty feet beyond where the boat came to a stop. To add insult to injury, there was a sailing schooner in view crewed by a bevy of high school girls who witnessed the entire spectacle and produced a rousing cheer in appreciation of Dick's performance. I presented my own support for Dick by lying facedown on the deck laughing hysterically until the loss of blood to my brain caused me to see red. Naturally the engine died and would not start afterward, requiring Dick to swim unceremoniously back to the boat amid cheering schoolgirls. But that's not the point. This is: my sister, Mary Ann, observed us soon after working on the boat to fix the leak once and for all. We really didn't know where the source of intrusion was, so we poured epoxy here and there hoping it would find its way to the proper spot. She asked why not flip the boat over and fix it on the outside, where it was more likely to be visible. Ha! Girls and their crazy notions! After she left, we did just that, and dammit, there was the leak source, caused by a delamination of fiberglass layers likely caused during a hard launch. To express our appreciation, we invited her fishing, and she had a comment about everything we did and wondered aloud at the seemingly illogical approach in our tactics. She asked, "Why put the bait below the sinker if the sinker is supposed to be sitting on the bottom?" And "Wouldn't keeping the hook off the bottom prevent it from getting fouled?" And other nonsense. The worst part was she caught more fish than the rest of us despite having never held a fishing rod in her life. In retrospect, she managed to restructure our proclivities and organize them into an experience that was a lot more productive and meaningful but still fun. In appreciation I bought her a brand-new fishing rod to be kept aboard the boat for her exclusive use whenever she should join us. Of course, she never got to see the rod, let alone use it, because on our very next outing it was dropped overboard during a "shark" dance that Dick performed for our nephew Stephen's and my entertainment. In Dick's defense, it is a difficult thing to dance on a rocking boat with a fishing rod in one hand and a live shark in the other. Who knew? Though my appreciation of Mary Ann's thoughtfulness lies forever hidden beneath the sea, it's more important that she knows that I love her, and there is nothing more valuable than being loved. Her attention to detail, which I had once viewed as trivial, transformed me.

MORAL: Effective program managers focus on the people, context, and systems as the main elements in their strategies and lead with compassion and orderliness.

* * *

THE TRANSFORMATION INITIATED THROUGH OUR program management endeavor enhanced not only our engineering department productivity but also the company at large. The benefits of effective program management reach far beyond the four walls of our company; it is the voice and persona to customers who have engaged us to solve their antenna problems. The successful program manager, I have learned, manages expectations and simply uses dates as points of reference. There is an important relationship linking the trail of communication and the time commitments that have been exchanged between supplier and customer. Tipping the balance in favor of either entity is a recipe for failure, as was demonstrated by our on-time delivery experience.

The success brought to engineering by implementing competent program management became a prototype for other departments as well, especially our underperforming machine shop. Taking a holistic approach, we transformed management of the shop from being strictly time-driven to instead observing an optimal balance of quality, cost, *and* time. Rather than pushing jobs through the shop, we were planning them through in a way such that everyone participating in the workflow process understood the scope of the work and their role in completing it. We stopped fretting over time and centered more on getting things right, tweaking here and there along the way until six-hour machining programs were reduced to three hours and so on. It took enormous dedication within the shop to effect these positive changes, and I don't want to oversimplify the effort that was carried out for this to succeed, but it was largely our new focus on program management that set us on the right path.

The assets, personnel, and machines of manufacturing we possessed throughout the transition we made during this period went essentially unchanged. What facilitated the transition from Micro-Ant as a sluggish company toward an efficient operation poised and ready for growth was our view of process and management. Our new focus on program management helped guide us to a better management team with the right people in the right jobs executing the right plans. The right plans are those that set appropriate priorities so that resources are placed where they are most profitable and effective. The right people are those who understand the plan, communicate it clearly, and follow through with the right measure of management until the goals are met. The right job is one where the responsibilities of the individual holding it are crisp and clear and relatable to the tasks necessary to facilitate the workflow process. The qualities that describe a good manager, plan, or goal have in common the element of trust. Without this, it will be a difficult task to find willing followers. It comes down to the program manager to institute the processes we come to trust.

CHAPTER 7

Succession

ACCORDING TO JIM COLLINS, AUTHOR OF *GOOD TO GREAT*, two key discriminators stand out for companies making the leap to greatness as opposed to the comparison companies that did not. These are related to the personality of the individuals leading the organization and where they came from. In the transitioning companies, leaders tended to be selfless, humble, even shy, taking almost no credit for the accomplishments of the company but quick to take responsibility for any shortcomings in performance. No surprise. The leaders of the comparison companies that did not make the transition were universally egocentric, taking credit for everything that went right and passing on the blame for anything that went wrong. They were also aggressive in their management styles and leaned toward threats over incentives as a means of encouragement. Again, no surprise. This is no great revelation as people are far more apt to rally behind the benevolent leader than the bullying bureaucrat. The less-expected aspect of the observation is where the successful leaders came from: within the ranks of the organization. It was discovered that leaders who rose to the executive position after spending ten years or more in tenure within the company workforce effected the successful transition from good to great, whereas those who were appointed from outside, despite celebrity status or extensive experience, tended not to. Understanding the inner workings of the company and its workforce trumps an impressive résumé. An insider respectful of the corporate culture succeeds whereas an outsider who never quite fits in will not. Experience or skill level are only minor factors in the outcome.

By adding depth when hiring employees, it should be no coincidence to find among your team the successors for every position within the organization right to the top. A good team places less demand upon a manager, who can succeed in that environment by exercising good judgment and being in touch with the nuances of the workforce culture. I am speaking directly from experience; I am an engineer with little knowledge of business, accounting, quality assurance, manufacturing management, and so on, yet we succeeded soundly because individuals far more capable than I filled the depths of our capability pool. You may have read a book or two about leaders and leadership, as I have. You may also have heard that good leaders are born, not made, or at least not made easily. I'm not a subscriber to this leadership concept per se but rather believe the employees ultimately make the decision whom they are going to follow, which is separate from whom they are obliged to report to. Leadership is about character, with sufficient doses of wisdom, experience, and capability. The leader *should not* take credit for the great things their company achieves. Instead, credit is due to the employees working beneath the leader, who merely inspired them to perform their very best. The leader *should* take responsibility for the shortfalls of their company because they have not inspired the team to do their very best. A bad strategy might play some role in this, but as we saw earlier with the on-time delivery stratagem, even the best-intentioned objectives fail miserably under poor leadership. If you have observed the recommendations from Chapter 2 in your hiring practices, then you should have a surplus of intelligence, work ethic, and capability overlap on your team. From this fertile environment, you will find the leaders of your tomorrow.

* * *

LIFE LESSON: Dick and I woke one morning to observe Mike perched over our heads atop the headboard of our bed, which doubled as a bookcase. Two things caught our eyes that aroused curiosity and suspicion. First, Mike was giggling that giggle that typically preceded some devilry. Second, he was entirely naked. Quicker than our ability to react, he began urinating on us, swinging his hips to and fro to form a sinusoidal stream to maximize coverage. Dick and I both knew if we were to exact justice upon Mike, it had to be done before he could escape into the protective forcefield of our mother, as he did in this case. Whilst the rest of us suffered the various hijinks of our older siblings, Mike was immune to it, finding shelter with Ma, which incited us to invoke fair play using other methods. Most effective was our singing of songs composed in his honor, such as "Lamentations of the Baby" or that timeless classic, "Michael, You Are a Baby." The torment we older boys endured was mostly physical, readily healed, whereas Mike was dealt the emotional variety, where the wounds are less easily detected. In our defense, it's all we had to keep him in check. As Mike grew older, we continued teasing him about various enterprises he would embark on, such as raising a farm. Dick would accuse him of taking animal husbandry too literally. And so on. Mike would eventually graduate with a master's degree in computer engineering, surpassing the rest of us in his technical skills and ability to employ them. Mike's professional time nowadays is split between managing his own small software/hardware business and filling a high-level executive position in a multi-national company supplying utility grade measurement equipment. Mike is the classic example of a quiet, understated force, moving through the ranks to eventually alight upon its perch, while the rest of us gaze in wonder and admiration. The irony, or perhaps justice, in this story is that Dick now reports to Mike, who is his manager. This allows Dick the unique distinction of having a manager who pissed on him, literally. As they say, it's better to be pissed off than pissed on, and Dick has been both.

MORAL: To find the great leaders of tomorrow, look first within your own ranks. If you hire right and manage well, this is where you will find them.

* * *

MICRO-ANT WAS FORTUNATE TO HAVE multiple candidates in its ranks to rise to the executive level. All had the correct disposition, were well-respected by the employees, and were dedicated to the success of the *entire* organization. Complementing this was a company culture and workforce deep in capability and meeting the three criteria mentioned earlier common to the very best employees and managers, i.e., *intelligence, work ethic, and submission to authority.* I never thought of myself as particularly gifted at leading until circumstances thrust me into the spotlight and forced me to decide whether to lead, follow, or get out of the way. My diffidence toward leading stemmed from my lack of formal training in business or in management. I assumed anyone claiming to have this experience automatically had skills superior to my own. In that case, it was best for me to stay out of their way. My predecessor in the president role enjoyed meetings almost to the point of obsession, whereas I had started viewing them as wasted time. One day he came into my office looking for me for the purpose of dragging me to a meeting, but I heard him stamping in my direction well in advance of his arrival, which allowed me ample time to hide under my desk so as not to be discovered. As I crouched under the desk, listening to him grunt once or twice before turning away, a thought took hold of me. What the hell am I doing? Here I am, the founder of the company, hiding like a hermit crab from somebody who ultimately reports to me. This was a low point for me and deservedly so because I was complicit in causing the haze of anxious sentiment that had taken over our company and its culture by allowing it to go on. It was time for me to come out from under the desk, metaphorically and literally, and take charge of a situation that was clearly not going well, yet was within my authority to assuage. It was not long after this incident that our then-president retired, and discussions began regarding who would take his place. Unsolicited and without counsel, I took the position. They say good leaders are born, not bred, and if so, I was born under a desk.

There were several factors pushing me to establish Micro-Ant's NextGen team before the end of 2021. Most obvious was that it simply makes logical sense to look forward in all aspects of the business, including corporate leadership, because like it or not we each come with an expiration date, and having a succession team in place is vital to the continued operation and growth of the company. Next, I did not want any potential private equity partners to be burdened with this effort or leave open the possibility of an ill-fitting person being appointed to a key position, thereby creating a negative impact on culture. As responsible leaders of the company, it was our duty to have some semblance of an exit strategy so that we could start planning our personal lives independent of the company and the company could plan for its future independent of us. By early August 2021, we had established a two-year plan that would promote existing employees to the positions of chief operating officer, chief technical officer, director of business development, and finally, president. These key leaders would, in time, along with others in the organization, become long-term stakeholders as partial compensation for the important roles they filled.

* * *

LIFE LESSON: At least once per week we would have wild rabbit for dinner, which Hank would bag with his .22 rifle in and around our many gardens. I was quite envious of this, but being too young to handle a rifle, had to resort to other weapons. This was sometime between learning to walk and attending first grade, when I would spend a good part of my day beneath our house, hunting rats. There was ample space to prowl around in this underworld, which included mounds of dirt, deep ditches, and a maze of sawed-off timbers that served as support columns. How my father cajoled my mother into making this hovel our home is a mystery to me, but many promises were likely involved. My gear consisted of a hunting arrow and a flashlight, which I would shine into the deep recesses of their dark domain, making the rats' eyes glow in the beam as they lined up to stare at me. I made many attempts to enlist our cat, Matilda, to join these expeditions, but she showed little interest in it. Despite my great efforts, I could not bag a single rat, as they proved too skittish to get within arrow-thrusting range. My attempts at baiting them closer with Velveeta cheese provided no result. Then one day, *paydirt*! Crawling within one of the deeper trenches, I came upon the granddaddy of all rats, dead stiff. I grabbed it by the tail and dragged it out, singing aloud as I went and exulting in my grand fortune. I could not wait to show my mother. She would love it! I headed into the house, holding my prize still by its tail behind my back, the head nearly dragging on the floor. In the kitchen were my mother and my sister. Oh, what a day! Bursting with pride, I yelled, "Guess which hand!?!" Too excited to wait for an answer, I followed up with, "THIS ONE!" In one swift motion, I swung my arm around so the rat could be displayed, but it seems a rat's tail is a difficult thing to grasp securely because it flew from my hand into the air, end over end, toward the stove, where an enormous pot of tomato sauce was cooking. The dancing and shrieking that took place in no way reflected the shower of accolades I had imagined.

My sister screamed, "GET IT OUT OF HERE!" My mother shrieked, "DON'T TOUCH IT!" This added to my confusion. Perplexed by their conflicting instructions, I ran out of there, leaving the rat behind. It made no sense. I saw Hank bring home many a rabbit, which ended up either in the tomato sauce or in the oven, and there was no shrieking involved. I guess it was simply not yet my time to succeed Hank as provider for the family dinner table.

MORAL: Good leaders are only as good as the team willing to follow them.

At present, Micro-Ant has a solid team of managers, and although each is relatively young, any one of them qualifies as the next person to lead our company as president. Several years ago, we founded a subsidiary of Micro-Ant called Kore Composites. Its tagline is "*Quality is a reflection of character.*" This is meant to indicate that we put our very best into the design and manufacture of Kore products and that its standards of quality are high. This same tagline applies to the people we employ. Our team is of the highest quality, possessing character traits that are essential to maintaining a 4S-worthy business. This is not by accident; as I have written, the importance of hiring people of good character cannot be overestimated. Remember, your employees today could be your leaders of tomorrow. I mean it. More than that, I've practiced it.

CHAPTER 8

Company CPR

IN SPITE OF YOUR BEST EFFORTS, SOONER OR LATER YOU WILL be faced with a crisis that interrupts, if not threatens, the fabric of your business. A crisis can manifest itself in many different ways, and there is no one-size-fits-all solution. But all problems have one thing in common: they need to be fixed. Crisis management takes cool, clear thinking, and your first priority must be the preservation of the company and the well-being of its employees. The actions I took to solve the predicament our company fell into are rather specific but still provide a lesson others might learn from and employ toward situations warranting immediate attention. Righting a listing ship is no easy thing, and it usually takes teamwork to set things right. One of the Life Lessons in this chapter is one of the worst I experienced in my life—and also one of my favorites. Left to our own devices, Dick, Mike, and I came so close to destroying our home. Only through sheer will and a determination to survive, we managed to invent a patchwork solution to the problem (though it found no favor with our mother).

The events that transpire in this chapter are what inspired me to write this book. The transition we made during this period in our history was remarkable to me and needed telling. Having worked as a nurse, I was no stranger to crisis management. But this was a different animal, and it had been a long time since I'd performed CPR on anyone. The first step in my overhaul strategy was to recognize what had happened. The second was to appoint myself as president and take charge. Stepping into the role of president, I had the sensation of living in a game of human whack-a-mole; one problem was fixed while another instantly popped up to take its place. My first instinct was, "*Oh shit, what have I gotten myself into?!*" But by taking small, decisive actions, I eventually resolved each of the issues I faced. During this period, my life's lessons provided guidance through situations that at the onset seemed both daunting and ridiculous.

At Micro-Ant, our Org chart is structured such that every department reports to the president, who in turn reports to the CEO. When the position of president was vacated by Scott, it left a gaping hole within the organization, leaving every department with no one to report to. The logical short-term solution was to have the CEO pick up this role, except Jim was already engaged in business development activities critical to the ongoing business. Still, I did not want to hire a replacement until we fully understood what brought us to this state.

A common complaint amongst our staff was that everyone felt inanimate, disconnected from the flow of operation, and confused by the ever-changing priorities set upon them. Everyone understood the message—deliver on time—but that was the extent of it. They felt punished to the point of being numb. In one-on-one meetings, I mainly listened. Some of these sessions ended in tears. Those of us on the executive level were not aware of this sentiment. We'd concluded instead that certain behaviors by certain people were largely to blame, and there was certainly truth in that too. But it made me wonder, what sort of organization were we to be utterly vulnerable to the misconduct of one (or even more than one) individual? The thought formed in me that we lacked a plan that would not only govern and standardize the execution of our job responsibilities but also keep wayward behavior in check.

The company was bleeding, and something needed to be done quickly to stem the flow.

* * *

LIFE LESSON: In a momentary lapse of judgment, my mother trusted me, Dick, and our younger brother, Mike, to manage the house while she attended to a family matter out West. It was the dead of winter, one of the coldest on record, so our mom left us ample money for heating oil and food. She issued one instruction—"Water my plants. Don't let them die."—and was off. Dick hit upon the idea that if we didn't use the furnace, we could spend the fuel money on more useful things. We promptly turned the furnace off to conserve fuel oil. There was a wood stove in the house, so the scheme was not entirely imprudent. However, each night got progressively colder, and the wood stove proved insufficient to the task of warming the house, which would have still been bearable except for listening to Mike whine all night long, "I'm cold. I'm so cold." We jointly decided to relocate the wood stove and ourselves into the barn, which had considerably less space to heat. The temperature dropped to minus thirteen degrees Fahrenheit that night, yet we slept cozy and warm, except for listening to Mike whine, "I'm hot. I'm so hot." Really. The next day I went into the house to use the bathroom and discovered the toilet water was frozen solid. So too were the sink faucets, and apparently so too were the hot water radiators located in each room. Dick turned the furnace on and set the thermostat to "hard over." Nothing. The radiators all remained ice cold. Not a problem. We brought the wood stove back in the house, but to accelerate the thawing process we did not connect the stove pipe to the chimney and instead let the heat, smoke and all, fill the house. It worked. To our chagrin, the first sign of water flow was from the living room radiator, which burst, embedding shrapnel into wood trim as far as fifteen feet away. The volume of water gushing from the gash is beyond my ability to articulate. It needed to be dealt with quickly. We knew there must be some shut-off valve somewhere but had no idea where to look. Armed with a few tools, Dick went into the dirt crawl space beneath the house, and after a short space of time filled with scuffling sounds and banging, the water flow completely stopped. He returned triumphant, announcing he'd hammered the copper water pipe feeding the radiator completely flat, thereby stemming the flow. The next two days were spent retrieving the radiator shrapnel and gluing the many pieces back in place such that the casual observer would see no evidence of our unfortunate mishap. Brilliant! But my mother did not see it that way. She returned home to find every last one of her plants dead from frostbite and then received an appraisal from a plumber estimating the cost of our "fix." On a positive note, we did save a fortune on heating oil, which was used instead to purchase a twelve-week supply of donuts from the bakery thrift shop.

MORAL: When managing a crisis, focus first on the cause before dealing with the effect. Fix the problem at the source. Any boater will tell you—don't bail until you find and plug the leak!

* * *

THE FLOW OF WORK WITHIN our company was inadequately controlled, intermittent, and ill-defined. There was no coherent plan that existed and was made visible to the team. Together with James, our chief engineer, and Tess, our CFO, we developed a workflow process that defined the steps to transition any product throughout the company from start to finish, from business development through engineering and eventually into production. It was quality assurance in practice, spelling out who was doing what. Plus, it was neatly tracked by our Materials Resource Planning (MRP) system. We presented the new workflow process to the employees, getting their input along the way, until we were satisfied with it. In time we gained the confidence to implement it. It established the proper management of corporate resources and put an end to misuse by those who tended to follow their own agendas. Perhaps most important, it cleared up the gray area that heretofore existed during handoffs between departments, making crystal clear the steps in the process necessary to ensure uninterrupted product flow.

We realized the benefits of the workflow plan within a few short weeks of implementing it. It streamlined the engineering development process and prevented engineers from being needlessly called to meetings or attending to issues that were entirely outside the scope of their responsibilities. This expanded design capacity, allowing the company to quote more opportunities, thereby increasing the volume of business that could be booked and executed. With the handoff between engineering and manufacturing clearly defined, a process that sometimes took weeks was suddenly accomplished in a matter of minutes, and the quality of the product-to-be improved because of the global understanding of its requirements. This is what I mean when I say that the plan is in essence "quality assurance in practice" because it facilitates adherence to the quality processes it is built upon. The workflow plan *is* a quality plan, and it ultimately leads to achieving scalability, meaning the capacity to grow.

Over the course of our on-time delivery experiment, QA had become a disenfranchised group of inspectors and repair technicians tied up with defect detection and troubleshooting returned merchandise. It was also bogged down in its own paperwork, seemingly meant to stall progress, not facilitate it. The view toward QA within the company was dismal. If a defective part escaped detection, it was QA's fault. If a unit was not properly assembled, it was QA's fault. If a product failed in the field, it was QA's fault. If a bird flew into the side of the building, it was QA's fault. A recurring sentiment of those I spoke with outside of QA was that QA was a liability and was dragging the company down, and there were endless examples to support it. We tasked our head of the QA department to develop a recovery plan that would get Quality Assurance back on track. As he struggled to develop a coherent plan that would complement our new workflow process, it became apparent that what was truly needed was a reset. A fresh directive that would stem the flow of defective parts escaping while not interrupting the flow of product. We met daily to discuss solutions until a plan was developed that would succeed. Expressed in the simplest terms, we agreed that Quality Assurance would focus on being process-oriented as opposed to object-oriented.

Before you say, "Hey wait! Quality is supposed to administer third-party inspection! How do you know the part blah blah blah...!?" and so forth, hear me out. The way I see it, the product is a physical realization of the process implemented to construct it. Get the process right and you get the product right. This "mind-on hands-off" approach is no different than what engineers practice when synthesizing the original design. Through the processes of geometry **designation**, electrical **simulation**, performance **optimization**, computer-aided drawing/design (CAD), and **documentation**, a *virtual* product is created and released to manufacturing that engineering may never see or touch. In fact, if we never hear about the product again once shipped, success! The success is in the process that created the product to be produced correctly. Why should QA not also succeed by being process-oriented instead of object-oriented or product-oriented?

Being process-oriented is being proactive, whereas being product-oriented boxes you within a reactive posture. From a QA perspective, being proactive equates to fixing the problem before it occurs, whereas being reactive equates to allowing the problems to occur and then dealing with them afterward. The enactment of this concept began with establishing a metrology group within the Operations Department and reassigning the QA inspectors to Operations. This one move shifted the responsibility of part inspection out of Quality and into Operations without compromising the standardized practices set by them. It also inserted Quality Assurance advocates into one of our most critical areas, where defects were most likely to escape. The real-time interaction between machinists and metrology inspectors facilitated the flow of quality practice *upstream*, allowing machinists to quality-inspect their own parts during fabrication, significantly reducing fallout from defects. Next, the responsibility of troubleshooting and subsequent repair of failed and/or returned parts was transferred to the line technicians who are trained and most capable of undertaking this sort of thing. No longer could employees complain that something was "stuck" in Quality Assurance. It was not possible unless that "something" was a process, and I've never heard of one of those gone missing. The number of employees within the QA department went from eight to *three*, while our product flow capacity increased as defects and failure escapes dropped precipitously. Now customer returns are almost unheard of, a thing of the past. When a part does escape, it is rarely without the prior knowledge of the operator facilitating the getaway. That is not a quality issue so much as a character issue, and those are more difficult to control but easy to spot.

LIFE LESSON: My brother Mike and I were hiking across an area of land that had been cleared some years before to make way for a housing development that never materialized. It was a good place to find box turtles, so our eyes were cast earthward, making us unaware of what we were walking into. We stumbled upon *three* white-faced hornet nests, all roughly at eye level (for a child) and buzzing lively with the stinging bastards. I screamed, *"Run!,"* which should have been self-explanatory, and executing my own advice, sprinted until out of danger. My elation at escaping unscathed was short-lived as I turned and saw Mike, barely moving at all, swatting both hands over his head in a pathetic attempt to shoo away the cloud of white-faced hornets diving at him. Oh, Mike! With a thousand possible actions to take, he chose the worst possible one! I had little option but to run back, pick him up from behind, and repeat my sprint, this time encumbered by Mike and a small swarm of pissed-off hornets. He was too groggy to walk, so I continued carrying him home, noticing that some hornets remained in his hair, on his arms, and under his clothes. Near our house was a pond, and I tossed him into it, thinking it would discourage the hornets from further pestering Mike. We reached home shortly after and reported to my mother what had happened. She produced the necessary antidote and called the doctor, who advised we keep an eye on Mike and not to let him fall asleep. Removing his clothing revealed attached hornets right down to the underwear, and we counted somewhere between fifty and seventy stings in total. The miraculous part of this encounter was that I did not receive a single sting, not a one. Even to this day I wonder how that could be and believe now that the hornets had no prejudice toward Mike over me but were intensely provoked by how he conducted himself. Perhaps the process of my escape indicated no threat, whereas Mike's lingering and handwaving presented a problem that needed dealing with.

MORAL: Your reputation as a business is largely dependent on your behavior as a person. The quality of any business relies on the quality of the people operating within it.

* * *

MY VIEW OF PRACTICING QUALITY is in many ways like health-care. In healthcare, you must always be on your guard against potential infection and have in place both preventative and remedial measures that minimize, if not eliminate, a negative reaction. A good healthcare practitioner educates the patient on measures of prevention so as to maintain good health but also prescribes treatments for symptoms following a diagnosis. Similarly, the quality professional educates operators in the quality processes that ensure good quality, i.e., product compliance, but also prescribes corrective measures for situations where inspection determines a diagnosis. The ultimate objective is to create a culture of quality—self-disciplined employees adhering to the quality processes set before them.

With QA now focused on implementing and managing workflow processes, there remained a need to deal with high-level Quality concerns like International Organization of Standardization (ISO) and Quality Assurance for Aerospace Systems (AS) certification compliance, vendor qualification, and development of a company-wide culture in sync with quality values. The transformation we made in the span of two months was nothing less than astonishing. It must be noted that we accomplished this with the very same personnel that were in place before problems began—the same ingredients but with a revised recipe. We had both the personnel and technology already in place to succeed; we had just been using them the wrong way.

* * *

LIFE LESSON: At very young ages, Dick and I had a keen interest in chemistry. Not because we were aspiring chemists, but because we had a fascination with fire. There were two elements and one compound we fixated on: carbon, sulfur, and potassium nitrate, the ingredients for gunpowder. Over time, we developed a mixture ratio that could be ignited and sustain a flame but that mostly generated smoke. This was a low-grade product, and we sought a solution that would explode. We experimented with ratios and texture, getting the powder as fine as possible by careful grinding, sifting, and blending. Still no explosion. Dick suggested mixing the powder with water to form a paste, which, when dried, did indeed explode. Success! We managed to blow a hole through the ice of a frozen pond with the first batch. But it took twenty-four hours for the paste to dry out before becoming serviceable gunpowder. It would be years until we hit upon a solution that accelerated the drying process. My mother brought home a new-fangled invention called a microwave oven. It could boil water in one minute and heat a TV dinner in two. Unfortunately, the device provided no guidance for drying out sixteen ounces of gunpowder, so to be cautious we set the timer to one minute and pressed Start. Almost instantly, it burst into bright flame, and black acrid smoke filled the kitchen. Neither Dick nor I dared get close enough to turn it off, and since Mike could not be goaded into it, we just let it play out. There was no disguising what had been done, even if Mike hadn't ratted us out. The good news was the microwave oven still operated though the interior was permanently scorched. Undone by technology, we never made gunpowder again. Too bad. It was our best batch.

MORAL: The quality of your resources is important, but success comes from your ability to manage them effectively.

CHAPTER 9

Implementing Scalability

IT IS ONLY NATURAL THAT A WELL-MANAGED COMPANY THAT finds its products in high demand will eventually consider how to expand operations. If you have abided by the fourth of the 4Ss, *scalability*, then this should not be overly difficult. Deciding on *how much* to expand, on the other hand, takes careful thought. Practicing scalability means you have a plan in place by which an increase in assets will have a predictable effect on productivity. For example, if one person using one mower requires two gallons of gas to do three lawns per day, then it might be expected that nine lawns per day will take a crew of three, each with a separate mower, burning a total of six gallons of gas. This is a bit oversimplified but helps illustrate the point. You must be aware of the productivity of your capital equipment (the lawn mowers), your human resources (the work crew), your utilities (the gas), and your production rate (three lawns per day). There will also be miscellaneous costs to budget for, like transportation to and from the work sites, maintenance for the mowers, and various administrative costs, all of which can be easily quantified and factored into your overall operational cost. Will serving three times the customers in this manner result in a 3X growth of the business? Not necessarily, especially if you have to borrow, at interest, to purchase the mowers or you have to service this larger operation by hiring another individual and so on. But it still sounds good in theory and will most likely pay off.

What about a more sophisticated operation supplying a variety of services, products, or both? The computations in this case need to be more precise even though the category of assets is not much different. Capital equipment, human resources, utilities, and service costs are still there along with admin costs, but now you have to account for the cost of unfinished goods, storage space, and handling and tracking these assets. Again, this is not difficult and should not deter you from expanding. A qualified accountant can predict your scalability based on the information you provide regarding your current production rate.

What *should* deter you from expanding, or at least give pause until more fully vetted, are the needs that come with such growth. Do you have the necessary experience on staff or access to a pool of competent candidates to manage a larger operation? Do you have a quality assurance program in place? If not, will you need one? Will your current facilities adequately serve the newly expanded operation? And so forth. Start by modifying your Org Chart so it reflects the operation after expanding. Talk to people qualified to fill the new positions you've outlined, and ask their opinion on how to proceed with each aspect affected by your projected growth. Once you've done this, you are ready to proceed. Get your growth plan on paper. You will need this if you plan to borrow money for the expansion. Your growth plan will likely resemble your original business plan, and it should because it is, in fact, a business plan. The key difference is that your growth plan will be built on your proven success as a growing enterprise, an extension of the business that began with your vision.

Micro-Ant has always been blessed with an abundance of business opportunities, aided in no small part by practicing blue ocean strategy, which means taking advantage of a market space where competition has become increasingly scarce. We were now primed to scale our operation from being good to being great. Good to great is a concept identified by Jim Collins, author of the book *Good to Great*, which describes the key factors that transform a good company into a great one. These include having disciplined leaders, practicing disciplined thinking, and cultivating a culture of self-disciplined employees. Collins's definition of *great* means sustaining a revenue growth over a period of years that outperforms the stock market by some multiple greater than two. That was Micro-Ant. In fact, our performance over the past few years, despite our missteps, well exceeded the market, so potentially, things were ripe for our transition.

In the fall of 2019, sixteen years distant from the humble basement operation, we were poised and ready to take the company to unimagined heights. A confluence of factors affecting our business had converged like a perfect storm. We were decisively functioning as a team coached to win and working toward an objective we all believed in against the backdrop of a culture steeped in optimism. Our capabilities portfolio had grown immensely and contributed to a reputation of being the best in our industry, leading to still more business opportunities. From a revenue perspective, our customer base transitioned from being disproportionately weighted toward a handful of products to a well-balanced, diverse portfolio of "Who's Who" companies in the commercial, aerospace, and defense sectors. To cap things off, emerging technologies and increasingly stringent performance requirements imposed by the FCC and other regulating agencies within the communications sector left us with far less competition and far more business opportunity. Like low-hanging fruit, it only awaited harvesting. We were good to go—good to grow. The first step was to set a performance goal, one that could be achieved without breaking what we had created but could evolve us into an even *greater* company.

We set a goal of increasing revenue 25 percent in 2020 by means of increasing product volume but not pricing. If anything, pricing should decrease due to the subsequent economy of scale we and our customers would both benefit from. Had someone forewarned us that the coronavirus pandemic was in the process of descending upon us, we would not have altered our plan one whit. McCarrick's Law had already taught me that if things could go wrong, they already had, so there was no sense in grousing about it while the nation's economy fluctuated around us as state and local governments shut down small businesses, especially those they deemed non-essential. For more details on this topic, read *The War on Small Business* by Carol Roth.

Our technology is a critical component within a supply chain that serves many essential users, that is, businesses of the large and influential variety, many of whom ordered us not to shut down during the COVID-19 crisis. In fact, demand for our products spiked during this period, and we were obliged to meet it with nearly half our workforce working remotely. The onus was put upon the manufacturing team to keep product flowing out and revenue streaming in. As a company, we were constantly concerned about becoming infected, causing a halt in operations and shutting us down as well as the many customers who rely on our product. Every possible precaution was taken to stay healthy, physically and economically. As the pandemic rose to its peak, so did customer demand for our products. We had more business than we could handle so we doubled down on our precautions against COVID-19. As many businesses struggled during this unfortunate time, we were growing, adding to our employee workforce, and posting uncharacteristically high production output. The goal we set out for the year was ambitious, but we were ready to meet it and now had all the elements of *scalability* in place.

* * *

LIFE LESSON: Not long after the gunpowder incident, Mike brought to our attention an advertisement for a mail order weather balloon, eight feet tall! Lower on the same page was an ad for a two-man submarine, but the $19.95 price tag was beyond our budget. In about six weeks, the weather balloon arrived, and we thought they had mistakenly sent us a package of those disposable toilet seat covers you see in public restrooms. Turns out that was what the balloon was made of. Once unfolded, separated into panels, and glued together, it was indeed a balloon and eight feet tall at that. We transported this fragile, weightless assemblage outdoors with the same delicate care as if it were the Shroud of Turin. Once outside in a light breeze, it filled with air and billowed into shape. Dick pointed out that this was good, but you know what would be great? If we filled it with hot air and sent it airborne. (It was, after all, a weather balloon.) We lit a fire using newspaper in a barrel customized with a funnel-shaped chimney top so that the hot air would direct into the balloon, which Dick and I held above it. With hot air filling the balloon, it soon formed that classic weather balloon shape, near ready for service. Mike started yelling, "Let go!" We ignored him because it was not quite filled to capacity and was thus premature. But when Mike's yells turned to screams of "FIRE!" we looked up in curiosity to find the top of the thing in flames and promptly let go. The screams of "Fire" aroused our neighbor, Amir, who came outside to witness. He was fascinated with our activities and would often stick his head over the fence separating our two backyards whenever he sensed some scheme afoot. As the balloon lifted skyward in an enormous ball of flame, we could hear Amir say between shrieks of laughter, "That doesn't look right. Deekie. That doesn't look right." Amir possessed a keen eye. The thing rose to maybe thirty feet before descending onto the field behind our house, which ignited in flames, it being the dry season. We foot-stomped the blaze out, declaring the whole experiment a great success. Mike remained disappointed that we'd destroyed his balloon. We countered that it was his fault for not speaking up earlier as he'd been on fire watch.

> **MORAL:** An ambitious goal requires an equally ambitious and well-managed plan, so do not take your eye off the ball(oon) once it is set in motion lest it go up/down in flames.

* * *

THE FIRST STEP TOWARD OUR growth goal was to reevaluate the company and our supply chain to assess whether sufficient resources were in place to meet the increase in product demand. We emphasized growing the capacities of our in-house machine shop and its counterpart, the production floor. There were serious deficiencies in these departments that needed addressing; both were already struggling to keep pace with current demands. In the case of the machine shop, we were deficient in milling machines that were "hands-off/lights-out," capable of producing parts around the clock with minimal intervention, save the occasional reloading of raw stock, which was generally bulk aluminum. Additionally, we had a tendency toward not properly employing the newer machines capable of volume production, reverting instead to the more familiar models that operated much slower and were incapable of production in any sense. Jim played a major role in upgrading the shop by identifying milling machines far more advanced than those we had been using and better suited to achieving the precision tolerances necessary for our products to perform. The solution was two-fold: (1) sell off the slower, less accurate equipment to make room for the new machines and thereby eliminate the temptation to use them, and (2) install a cluster of high-speed milling centers capable of producing precision parts in volume. The addition of the new equipment and the utilities to support them required a modest expansion of the machine shop, but the eight-thousand-square-foot warehouse space in which it was housed was already accounted for. The only option was to expand into the production space, which was already at capacity. We needed more space.

Relocating the production floor meant finding space offsite within near enough range of the current facility so as not to cause a commuting hardship for our workers. Moving an operation like this is no easy task and requires careful planning. The production department shared twelve thousand square feet of warehouse with two enormous antenna chambers plus office space for engineering and admin personnel and their activities. Not only would it be necessary to relocate the production floor, but we also needed to expand it in the process to meet increasing demand for our products. We needed a new building.

The new building, which we dubbed Micro-Ant East, was a three-floor facility with fifteen thousand square feet per floor for a grand total of forty-five thousand square feet, situated on a two-acre parcel of land with ample parking. We "won" it in an online auction where Jim put in the winning bid, which also happened to be the minimum threshold. We got it for well under valuation, which is always good, and its location reduced the commute for most of our employees—also good!

The first floor and a portion of the second floor were allocated to production and its related operations. The rest of the second floor was used for office space, meeting rooms, and general workspace, including labs for testing and delicate assembly. Now the third floor, which amounted to one-third of the total occupiable space, was dedicated to the employees and boasted an exercise gym, a lecture hall, an authentic café serving barista-quality lattes and homemade baked goods, and a cafeteria! WAHOO! I always dreamed of having a cafeteria because, let's face it, if your company has grown to the size where it needs a cafeteria, you've done *something* right. At this point, I could go on and on describing the countless hours I personally spent experimenting with different coffees and brewing methods and the many more hours I spent perfecting recipes for cream puffs, bagels, and the like that were sugar-free, gluten-free, and nut-free yet tasted every bit as good as you could want. We had in our employ a professional barista, and the wife of one of our engineers roasted coffee as a side business, which made having a world-class in-house coffee shop our apparent destiny. Given our attitude toward culture, it should come as no surprise that we would invest in and dedicate so much space and so many amenities to our employees. This recreational and social area was as much an investment as a luxury—a common place for all to talk, share ideas, and just have fun. The new building embodied so much of the culture, attitude, and well-being of the Micro-Ant family that it seems unfair to simply call it a building. It is more aptly described as the realization of a vision, a dream coming to fruition, a place of love and respect.

* * *

LIFE LESSON: Bill had several attributes peculiar to a cat. For example, he possessed nine lives and the cat-like ability to leap straight up to surprising heights. He once conducted a demonstration of these two traits to my everlasting astonishment. It began with Hank in his bedroom instructing our sister, Mary Ann, on gun safety. Hank had just told her that one should always make sure the chamber is empty before pointing a gun toward anyone and aimed the twelve-gauge shotgun he held at the bedroom wall. Instead of a benign click of the firing pin, an explosion erupted that reported to anyone interested that a spray of lead shot had just been discharged. Dick, Mike, and my mother were watching television. I was sitting at the dining room table adjacent to the kitchen, where Bill was putting something into a bowl on the counter. Bill stood facing the wall that divided Hank's bedroom from the kitchen, his midsection positioned toward ground zero. The lower cabinet doors at his feet were blast open, projecting out various contents that had been stored within. Bill leapt impossibly high and hung there for an instant as though straddling an invisible horse. His response appeared to be instantaneous with the blast, such that if Hank had forewarned, *"Get ready, Bill, I'm gonna shoot through the wall at you,"* his execution could not have been timed more perfectly. Bill never lacked urgency, especially if responding quickly was imperative. The contents of the cabinets lay strewn about the kitchen floor, save a glass jar of Kandy Korn, which sat still intact in the cabinet, unbothered by the blast, confirming its indestructibility and infinite shelf life. Bill stood in the middle of this debris field unscathed, bowl in hand, managing to have alit perfectly on his feet, like a cat.

MORAL: Successful leaders react quickly and with purpose. When challenges arise, they are thrilled for the opportunity to act.

* * *

THE FOCUS OF THIS CHAPTER, of course, is scalability, the fourth of the 4Ss. Growth of a company can happen so quickly you might feel yourself operating in reactive mode. This is fine, but as pointed out in the previous Life Lesson, reaction must be executed with purpose. If your ambition is to grow, then planning ahead for it will go a long way toward making your expansion one that is controlled and commits minimal casualty to the organization. Micro-Ant's growth was a bit like holding a tiger by the tail, but hold on we did—and tightly. We all managed to come through it intact and better for the experience. As we went through the various scenarios described in this chapter, I was ever mindful of how corporate objectives affected our culture. Moving to the new building created a challenge I hadn't foreseen, but once I realized what was going on, I was able to remedy the issue. As we moved the various operational groups one at a time, those left behind quickly felt disconnected, and I began getting reports of low morale. Some employees even began looking for new jobs. The move was taking too long, and uncertainty began to brew amongst the team. I had not done a good job of communicating the urgency of getting us all under one roof, instead putting more emphasis on avoiding operational disruptions rather than keeping people happy and connected with the company culture. Things got to the point where I traveled to the old building and spent the day talking to every employee there one on one, much as I did when managing the on-time delivery crisis. It was a Thursday, and my promise to the employees was that they would relocate on Monday and should report to the new building for work after the weekend. This was a bold goal to be sure, perhaps even a bit ridiculous given the complexities associated with moving assembly line assets and getting them all up and running again, but I had several things going for me. First, our production teams work four ten-hour shifts and take Fridays off, so that gave us three full days to accomplish the move. Second, the team in place for executing the move was highly capable for such tasks and loyal to my instruction. Third, I had HR send out a company-wide email that all production personnel were to report to the new building come Monday because their jobs no longer existed at the old one. If that doesn't light a fire under a person's ass to get moving, then not much else will. Come Monday, the move was indeed executed, and with everyone under one roof sharing the same dream, we were a single team again, a happy culture of industrious workers.

As a business *owner*, you really don't want to spend much time in reactive mode. It's better to be proactive so as not to lose authority and control. As a business *manager*, you will no doubt find yourself operating in reactive mode when you are attempting to rectify situations that moved quicker than you planned, or perhaps not as quickly. The important thing is *how* you respond. It must be quick, decisive, and, of course, with the greater good in mind. The fabric of the company must always be preserved, and that should be your guiding priority in all the objectives you set, in the strategies you execute, and most of all, in how you manage your team.

CHAPTER 10

Transition

AS EARLY AS THE INITIAL DAYS OF LAUNCHING MICRO-ANT, inquisitive parties would ask me, *"What is your exit strategy?"* My knee-jerk response to this question was, *"I don't know, but hopefully I'll have some choice in the matter."* Twenty years later, I still don't have anything in place that would fit the definition of a formal exit strategy, and that does not concern me one whit. The one certainty I have is that one day my employment at Micro-Ant will be terminated, but until that day comes, my focus must be on making the company strong and *hyper*-sustainable, with a team in place capable of carrying the torch forward. If I were to leave the company today, the biggest question facing me would be, *"What do I do now with all this spare time?"* rather than, *"What will happen to the company I'm leaving behind?"* If I were to sell my shares of the company in an acquisition, however, the purchasing party would very much be interested in what the operation will look like if I leave and would likely want me to stay on staff for three to five years, or even longer. I know this because I've had this discussion with a number of parties interested in acquiring Micro-Ant, and if anything, I am somewhat flattered by their assessment of my value to the operation. Truth is, I expect to do this another ten years or so, acquisition or no, continuing to grow and strengthen the company to provide job opportunities for many years to come. With my personal transition plan, exit strategy, whatever, so ill-defined, I can provide little guidance to those contemplating their own departure. For me, the important thing is that the company will continue to operate and maintain its good reputation and legacy. So, my exit strategy is focused on the preservation of the company rather than what I do with my spare time. Here is my question for those considering their exit strategy plan: what will the company look like without you?

There are basically three answers to that question: (1) it continues to operate under new management; (2) it is completely dismantled and auctioned off; or (3) it is acquired by a third party who takes over operations. As a business owner, option three will likely be the most appealing because it allows you to maintain your legacy and also cash in on your nest egg. At the time of this writing, there are no acquisition activities taking place at Micro-Ant, but the mechanics of the process are being explored. I believe it to be sound thinking to have this option on hand—but also responsible thinking because this could be a key strategy for keeping the company intact, with or without you. If we do end up selling Micro-Ant, I won't hide it from the employees. That much I know.

* * *

LIFE LESSON: My Nonnie would sometimes come stay with us, and one day she arrived with a giant steamer trunk. We boys quickly realized that more interesting things besides clothes could be put in the trunk, such as the provisions necessary for a voyage to Mars or an Atlantic crossing. One day, a most fascinating scene took place with the trunk at its center. Hank suggested a game in which we took turns locked in the trunk for sixty seconds. He offered himself first in. We had long broken the latching mechanism, so it required someone to sit on the lid to discourage premature evacuation. Bill and I sat on the trunk as Hank counted to sixty, concluding with, "Okay, let me out." I slid off, but Bill enacted a variation to the game that involved *not* letting Hank out of the trunk. Realizing what was at play, Hank's tone became urgent, and in time he issued a variety of threats to be conveyed were he not immediately "Let. Out. Of. This. God. Damned. Trunk!" That was all good with Bill but not with me, for as far as Hank knew I was complicit in Bill's twist of the rules. Then Hank went quiet and, mastering his emotion with incredible composure, said, "Bill, *please* let me out of the trunk." This had an intense effect on Bill. The use of the word *please* rattled him. It was used so seldom between us boys that its definition was virtually unknown. Bill was in a dilemma and needed an exit strategy that likewise facilitated Hank's. He could not get off the trunk and escape as Hank surely would catch up and deliver on his promise to beat him. If he let Hank out voluntarily, same scenario. He began negotiating with Hank: freedom in exchange for immunity. "Do you promise not to beat me up if I let you out?" *"I do."* "Do you promise *to God* you won't beat me up?" "I *do*." Their exchange had all the formality of a wedding, and it should be noted that God was invoked not once but thrice in the trunk incident: first to damn it, second to open it, and third as a promise of salvation. With a promise to God sealing the deal, Bill opened the trunk and immediately received a fist in the eye. From my vantage point, it was like a Hank-in-the-box but without the windup music. Though Bill protested, it could not be a binding contract without a witness or other verification, since I elected to keep my mouth shut and a shiner in our house was circumstantial evidence at best.

MORAL: Once you start feeling like you're boxed in, it's time to think of an exit strategy. It need not be elaborate, but try not to leave any black eyes in your wake.

* * *

IN JANUARY OF 2020, GREG, Jim, and I were the sole shareholders of the company, and we considered our options as we looked toward the future. We each had differing personal situations to consider, but we all agreed that our priority was the preservation of the company and its continued success as a center of excellence providing well-paying jobs for years to come. We agreed too that for the right price, we would sell our shares in the company, allowing us each to enjoy sooner rather than later the fruits of our toil toward making the company a success. We jointly decided on a selling price that was decidedly fair and realistic. Jim, acting as our broker, believed he could get even more than this price and would make efforts to do so.

Upon compiling a brief containing financial information and a capabilities portfolio that might pique a potential buyer's interest, Jim set about talking to private equity investors and other business entities familiar with our industry. His goal was to establish a value for the company and to narrow down the field of well-suited candidates to engage in an acquisition. Jim informed us that it would take a period of one to two years to select an appropriate investor-partner to whom we could sell the company. Greg asked whether there might be an option to expedite the sale of our shares, and Jim proposed that he and I purchase Greg's interest valued pro rata in accordance with the figure we mutually agreed on. To this he readily agreed, and in a separate conversation he shared with me that the early payout appealed to him for personal reasons despite an opportunity to share in a higher selling price. Jim and I now turned our eyes toward the future, seeking out an investor that would partner with us in growing the company to its full potential.

Although we had been approached many times over the years by would-be suitors interested in our acquisition, we saw mostly corporations who would break the company by carving out only the part of our business that suited their interests. As may be expected, some of these were our very customers, so the potential conflict this would raise with our other customers had to be carefully considered and not ignored. Just as one would do a 4S self-assessment at the onset of a new venture, so should it be done for a potential partner. Do they have qualities that align with yours and contribute to the success of your business, or will there be conflicts that disrupt the wheel of fortune? We established a set of criteria meant to filter out prospective partners not meeting our fundamental requirements. The *right* buyer would:

- *provide more than just money in the transaction;*

- *acknowledge and preserve our culture;*

- *not increase prices to customers solely for the purpose of raising the bottom line;*

- *not practice strategies biased toward/against a particular customer or market segment;*

- *value the company at earnings before interest, tax, depreciation, and amortization (EBITDA) × N, where N is a fair multiple commensurate with our position in the market;*

- *not burden the company by leveraging it to pay off the owners; and*

- *allow us to continue in our roles, over some period, to ensure continuity.*

If even one of these criteria was not met, we would simply dismiss that entity as being ill-suited. Establishing these requirements was for the most part self-explanatory and perhaps obvious, but many acquisitions fail from not abiding by these simple tenets.

The requirement of bringing more than just money in the transaction was to ensure that the buyer would participate in the company's ongoing growth and development in the years ahead. The next three requirements should be self-evident as they focus on maintaining relationships that exist between the company and its constituents, which include employees, vendors, and customers. The multiple on EBITDA the acquiring company agrees to pay not only indicates their appreciation of the value of the company but also their expectations on how it will perform and the level of commitment toward succeeding they shall apply going forward. If the company must be leveraged to pay off the current owners, oh boy have you picked the wrong partner. It puts the company in a disadvantaged state financially and at risk generally.

Adhering to these criteria considerably narrowed the field of suitable buyers. Jim instructed our controller to have the past several years of financial statements audited to facilitate a well-defined and expedient due diligence process. Based on this data, he performed his own valuation of the company in which he included our annual expenditures toward research and development back into our EBITDA as these were a voluntary expense. Settling on a minimum N multiple satisfactory to the partners completed our readiness to entertain a deal should the right suitor come calling.

Early on we were approached by an equity group interested in purchasing our business. An internet search revealed that they had a portfolio of twelve companies similar in size to Micro-Ant and that a number of these had been held for many years, indicating this potential buyer was not in the flip-it business but rather a partner for the long haul. Additionally, each portfolio company maintained the same executive and management team post-acquisition, which aligned with our condition of maintaining continuity in management for some period of time. The more financial information we shared, the more they liked us, and by all accounts it appeared a deal would soon be struck. In fact, we were scheduled to meet in the firm's DC office to receive their proposal around the time that COVID made travel to such destinations impractical, if not impossible, so the meeting never occurred. With more important things going on in the world, talks of acquisition were postponed and for the time being forgotten. For our part, Jim felt that it was for the best because we were on a growth trajectory despite the ensuing pandemic, and we could expect a much higher valuation once we came out on the other side of it.

***

EVEN DURING THESE EARLY PHASES of acquisition, we kept the managers informed of our intent, appraised them of what to expect moving forward, and prepared with them a transition plan structured to have minimal operational impact. Our objective was to have the very same people responsible for making the company a success continue in their roles. This was in sharp contrast to the Seavey acquisition, which ignored how the employee base might be affected. Their foremost concern was adding to the bottom line by reducing overhead. Our employees have always come first and are secure in that knowledge. As much as we wanted our team to be aware of these activities, we did not want any of this to be a needless distraction either. There was so much going on during this time that we could hardly spare even one set of eyes off the ball. For example, we were launching a whole new product line that we had spent two years developing internally and were diligently working on a new website and marketing campaign, having engaged the world-renowned Tony Felice Agency to oversee this branding effort.

A transition of leadership is often accompanied by a sense of anxiety, especially in those feeling left in the dark to ponder what the future might bring. In many cases these anxious feelings are based on stories recounting acquisitions gone horribly wrong, with loss of jobs and culture shock. It is like a modern-day telling of *The Goose that Laid the Golden Eggs* in which accountants choke the living creativity out of an organization to save a dollar here and there. This may not seem a fair assessment, but it is exactly the tactic Pradeep took during the Seavey acquisition. I want to re-emphasize here that I did not part ways with Seavey because Pradeep wanted to reduce my salary by twenty thousand dollars. I left because he did not care about me or anything to do with the business beyond what he could squeeze out of it. As you navigate through the acquisition process, exercise prudence and due diligence to ensure the new owner fits your policies and code of ethics. Change is inevitable but not entirely out of your control. When Micro-Ant was considering its options for a sale, we became well acquainted with each potential buyer and moved away from those we did not see as a good fit.

* * *

LIFE LESSON: On a bitter cold New England day, I set out with Hank, Bill, and Dick to a convenience store that was roughly four miles from our home. I was not appraised of the purpose of our shopping expedition, but that was not unusual. Plus, I didn't really care. It was so cold that the normally flowing brook that ran beneath the overpass we were crossing appeared frozen over, so we all went down to investigate. Either by happenstance or intent, Hank and I ended up on one side of the stream with Bill and Dick on the other. It was soon decided, with no input from me, that I should form my body into a torpedo and be thrust across the frozen brook to test a theory. *Earlier in this book, when I justified my reasoning for throwing Hank and Bill's fish down the drainpipe, this is the sort of thing I was talking about.* I removed my jacket as instructed to minimize friction and then effected the posture of a compact human torpedo as Hank sent me gliding across the ice into the receiving arms of Bill and Dick. I was quickly spun around, pointed toward Hank, and again set into motion. I was no rocket scientist but understood propulsion dynamics enough to know that Bill's thrust was insufficient for a successful ice crossing. I suddenly found myself stalled halfway across. From both banks came shouts of conflicting advice, seemingly meant to put me under the ice, not across it. I recall staring straight through the crystal-clear ice into the depths below, trying to make out the bottom but unable to see it. Since I was already facing in that direction, I opted for Hank's bank and made sweeping motions with my arms as though doing the breaststroke as per his recommendation. Hank had his arm stretched out, as I did mine, until our hands were very near touching. With salvation so near at hand, I became anxious in my mind and ambitious in my kicking, breaking through the ice and ending up on the wrong side of it. When people tell you that falling into freezing water is like being stabbed with a thousand needles, they know what they're saying. Rescue was executed by Hank, who grabbed hold of my hair and lifted me out of the brook. I was wet and cold but soon just cold because my wet clothing quickly froze into a cardboard suit. Thankfully my jacket was unaffected since I'd removed it at the onset. None of this, by the way, deterred us from finishing our trip to the convenience store. I have no recollection of what was purchased or why, but my journey there will never be forgotten.

MORAL: As in any adventure, the journey is every bit as important as the destination.

* * *

BY MID-SUMMER OF 2021, WE had narrowed down the field of prospective buyers to three. One bidder stood out by extending a significantly higher offer, which amounted to an evaluation of the company approximately thirty million dollars higher than the other two. The company making the highest bid was another antenna company whose offer included, among other things, to purchase Micro-Ant for a price almost equal to ten thousand times what Pradeep tried to cut my pay by. How can you say no to an offer like that!? Well, we did end up saying no. After looking more closely at the culture and business strategy of that organization, it became clear to us that merging the two companies would be an ill fit, and the net result would be one company sapping the resources from the other. An extra thirty million in the pocket did not sway us one way or the other because it wasn't only about the money. Jim and I wanted to preserve the great thing we'd created and keep it going. I suppose I should thank Pradeep for teaching me such a valuable lesson since he set into motion my dream of being an entrepreneur and the company that resulted from it.

Retirement is something I've never contemplated. I expect when I do retire, it will be imposed by force majeure as opposed to a choice. Instead, I am always looking toward the next thing and am fortunate enough to consider ventures that are profitable in a non-economic sense. When founding Micro-Ant, I made a point of not naming the company after myself, as the owner of a single-handed operation is tempted to do. My purpose in not having my name associated with the business was so that it would not be viewed as an extension of myself but rather as an enterprise standing upon a brand more than a name. Seavey Engineering, which was of course named after John Seavey, was always perceived in the industry as "John's company." When the company sold, the new owner wisely kept the same name because it was John Seavey's name and good reputation that alone kept the business on life support as it was slowly choked into obscurity. Once it became apparent that there was no longer a Seavey at Seavey, its loyal customers sought their antenna needs elsewhere, many coming to Micro-Ant. My expectation was always that we would grow far beyond reliance on any single person. When the day comes that the company operates equally well with or without my involvement, it is time to start thinking about that next thing. The days of thinking are upon me now, and the better I get at sewing and the more bags I deliver, the appeal is gaining for converting the Swordy Moon brand into an economically viable enterprise.

* * *

LIFE LESSON: Dick and I outfitted our canoe with a jib sail that came with a wooden sailboat purchased from a neighbor. We used a hollow aluminum pole that once served as a rooftop FM TV antenna for a mast and stabilized it with several strategically placed stays. The makeshift mainsail was outfitted with a permanent boom of thick-walled PVC to improve its effectiveness in catching wind. Steering was accomplished by pulling on a mainsheet to adjust the sail's position relative to the wind in conjunction with dipping a paddle for a rudder. In winter when the lakes froze over, we were struck with the idea of converting our sailing canoe into an ice sled. The apparatus consisted of a wooden frame of two-by-fours fashioned into an isosceles triangle, with a skate blade fixed at each vertex, the apex facing in the direction of travel. Dick and I differed in opinion on mounting the mast and sail, which is vital to the lesson of this story. Dick wanted to remove the canoe from the assembly, arguing that its additional weight would slow us down, whereas I wanted to keep it to stabilize the sail better and contribute to our safety should the ice prove too thin. This argument went back and forth, with Dick citing hydrodynamic principles and math-based logic. I simply didn't want to drown. We kept the canoe and transported it all to the largest natural lake in the state of Massachusetts, which is several miles across. The wind was fresh, so we cast off at an exhilarating pace that soon became frightful.

We learned that the mechanisms used to effect steering in water were ineffective on ice, and attempts to trim the sail were met with dynamics suggestive of a violent broach or a clobbering by a free-oscillating boom. Unable to stop, steer, or regulate speed in any way, we were committed to our enterprise. There was nothing to do but hang on for the three-mile crossing and see what should befall us as we met the approaching shore. Suddenly ahead in our direct path appeared a mass of open water, so we hung tight. Would we flip? Pitchpole? Break to pieces? We entered the water at ramming speed, dislodging the sled from the canoe as we did so, in the most controlled manner imaginable. Now in water, we regained control and corrected our direction, retrieved the sled, and pulled ourselves onto the ice, now facing back toward our original launching port. There was no sailing back as the boat preferred only a following wind, so we were obliged to dismast and tow it on foot. The decision to retain the canoe in the final design was a lifesaver, and I was happy not to have yielded to Dick's persuasive argument to the contrary.

MORAL: If you look back after having made your decision, you made the wrong one.

* * *

IN THIS CHAPTER, WE LOOKED at options you should consider when developing an exit strategy from the company you created. It seems like a mere handful of chapters ago we were trying to decide whether to start a company, and here we are now trying to decide how to leave it. So it goes. Although we focused on what happens to the company, we should also discuss what happens to *you*. Let's say you have come to the realization that the company can indeed operate independently of you and that you are ready to focus on the next phase of your life. You don't need to, nor should you, quit cold turkey. You can continue to consult in a diminishing capacity, set up and join a board of directors, or set up some side activity that supports the business in a meaningful way. Writing this book is one of those side activities for me, as is my increasing interest in launching Swordy Moon. I commandeered some space in the new Micro-Ant building and set up an operation with two industrial sewing machines and some experienced seamstresses to manage things. We call it the Fab Lab. Not only are we able to produce Swordy Moon Adventure Bags (SWAB) for donation and profit, but we also manufacture soft storage cases for antennas, which are sold to customers who also purchase Micro-Ant products. I can spend as much or as little time as my heart desires engaged in the Fab Lab, and one day I suppose it will become a full-time occupation for me.

How will I know when it is time for me to leave Micro-Ant as its president and chief science officer? Probably when I start asking myself that very question. That's when the rubber hits the road, and it's time to compile an exit strategy that defines both your departure from the company and how your time will be spent thereafter. Traveling, mentoring, and the like are all good options, but my advice is to preserve some measure of occupation that keeps you productive in mind and in body. If you have some sense of how you will occupy yourself going forward and you get to the point where you begin looking forward to it, then that is exactly what you should start planning for: going forward.

Leaving your company, your baby, your life's work is such a personal decision. I prefer to have that conversation with you in private. Peace.

CONCLUSION

Lessons Learned

IN THIS BOOK'S INTRODUCTION, I PROPOSED ADHERING TO four fundamental principles for starting and maintaining a successful business. These four principles are building blocks in a process I call the 4S Transform. The 4S Transform is employed as a self-assessment tool that provides budding entrepreneurs and established managers alike with a comprehensive look at the personal qualities and strengths within themselves and on their teams necessary to create a sustainable enterprise. The basic premise of the 4S Transform is that the success of a business can be traced back to the quality of the people comprising it and vice versa. Identifying and invoking these qualities up front offers a guide on how to transform your business into an organized, reputable company. I did not invent these principles, and to persons well read on business literature they might not be new or profound. But because I haven't seen them presented elsewhere in this methodical manner, I present them in this book for the purpose of serving other entrepreneurs as they have me.

The *4S*s, aka the four fundamental principles that must be incorporated for creating a sound business, are:

- *Salability*

- *Sensibility*

- *Sustainability*

- *Scalability*

I learned this concept only after making many costly mistakes, so I can personally attest to the benefit of having this knowledge available prior to making business decisions that might turn detrimental. Although possessing a high level of salability, I lacked the sensibility to monetize the many doors of opportunity open to me and thus saw profits going to customers rather than to my business. This is when my life experiences reminded me that almost any problem can be solved by thinking about it the right way. I had been looking at this problem the wrong way. Providing finished goods in addition to consulting services was a sensible first step toward generating recurring revenue and adding personnel to establish sustainability. The next steps were to develop a greater level of sensibility to structure even better deals and begin focusing on systems and processes to generate scalability and ongoing growth.

A business becomes sustainable once it grows beyond the reliance on any one individual to operate. This is different from financial sustainability, which is certainly an important requirement of owning a business but guarantees neither evolving value nor longevity. Building equity in a one-person operation is extremely difficult because there is little value in a company that can only be run by a single critical employee. This is also a roadblock to scalability, which is how a business grows. Since antenna engineers were in short supply, we were constantly on the lookout for professionals in the field we could add to our engineering team for sustainability and growth. My advice to anyone starting a business is to plan on adding human resources and operating equipment as early as the budget allows to ensure sustainability and to build equity. If your "business" consists solely of you and your lawn mower, then what you really have is not a business but a job. That's all well and good, until either you or the lawn mower quits. Then what?

***

LIFE LESSON: Someone please explain to me why young boys, at their own peril, are mysteriously drawn toward dangerous objects in motion, such as a trotting horse, Rocky Balboa, or my brother Bill pushing a lawn mower at breakneck speed up and down the driveway? The uniqueness of this childhood flashback is that it teaches the same lesson twice from two different perspectives. In the first, I was running parallel to the lawnmower at a speed my legs could not justify, barefoot and clad only in shorts. My path was on the side of the mower that had an outlet where rocks, stumps, and occasionally grass were discharged. It prudently featured a safety device consisting entirely of a child-sized hand painted just over the opening with a red *X* through it. Running along in this manner, I felt myself inexplicably drawn closer and closer to the mower's discharge, as though by some magnetic force, until my bare ankle contacted its razor-sharp steel perimeter, neatly shaving off a portion of the ankle skin and producing a flow of blood that left me too shocked to even cry. Dashing into the house and leaving a trail of blood in my wake, I found my mother, who lifted me into the kitchen sink to cleanse and bandage my wound. After I told her what happened, she said, *"I'll bet you'll never do that again."* She would have lost that bet, and quickly, because I immediately went back outside and encountered Bill, who had an expression on his face that I mistook for remorse. He invited me to sit on the lawn mower where it was "safe" and enjoy a leisurely ride. It was more of a directive than an offer but, more than anything, an opportunity to re-emphasize the lesson that had apparently been lost on me in the first go-around. Now, the unenlightened reader might wonder as to the necessity of running the lawn mower engine since Bill was providing the propulsion and no grass was to be mowed, but the throbbing sound of it invigorated Bill. Plus, the thought of a rotating propellor blade inches below my bare feet put the *thrill* in thrill ride. All was well and good on the straight segments of the run, but the hairpin turns forced me to cling to the hot engine for balance with an occasional jolt from the exposed spark plug electrode. Again, a reader untrained in such matters might question why there wasn't a rubber boot in place to insulate passengers like myself from this hazard. This is because the shut-off mechanism for the lawn mower consisted of a piece of spring steel that was mounted to the engine housing, which could be manually bent over to contact the spark plug electrode, thereby shorting it out to ground and arresting the spark needed for internal combustion to take place. Perhaps this was the apparatus that inspired my father to invent the electric frying pan with the detachable thermo-electro probe. Bill demonstrated to me that there was another option for shutting off the mower. Next to the driveway was a low area that tended to fill up with rainwater, at first producing a big puddle but over time a small pond. Floating upon this puddle pond was a picnic table, turned upside down to serve as a ferry for us boys. Tied to one of the ferry's legs was a rope, with its other end in a loosely tangled coil lying on shore. Bill was heading for the coil but must have decided the mower would not clear it, so gave one last heroic shove, either to get me across or get himself clear. The mower stopped short, propelling me up and forward, initiating an involuntary somersault. I dismounted smartly on my feet with all the grace and precision of an Olympic gymnast. My first sensation upon hitting terra firma was that I'd somehow shrunken six inches in height, and the fear of it fueled a dead run to the house, bandaged ankle and all. Whatever calamity had befallen Bill and the mower was of no concern to me in my state. This lesson had been taught to me twice now, and I did not want to repeat it a third time.

MORAL: Everyone comes equipped with an entire portfolio of lessons learned. Let yours be your guide toward succeeding at whatever goal you aim for.

* * *

ONCE YOU'VE SURROUNDED YOURSELF WITH people of sufficient good qualities on *both* sides of the transaction, as I like to say, now form them into a team. This begins with good leadership, with a clear objective, and a good strategy for achieving it. Once the right team is in place, even if it's just one other person, *scalability* and therefore sustainable growth is now possible. Again, it is vital that you have both a clear objective and a cogent strategy for uniting your team toward a common goal everyone believes in. Think back to the *on-time delivery* strategy versus the *one customer one product* strategy. Both appear reasonable at face value, but each led to polar opposite outcomes. The former produced a deleterious effect on our company culture and profitability whereas the latter spawned a team of high-performing superstars whose products are recognized worldwide as being outstanding and unsurpassed. So, what's wrong with delivering on time? *Nothing!* It was the manner of its execution that was the problem. The strategy for accomplishing on-time delivery was never developed into a cogent plan that could be succinctly communicated to the team and embraced. If the strategy to all such objectives is work harder, work faster, where is the incentive? If the reward is "not failing," as it was in this case, what sort of team spirit do you suppose would rise in response to this? Treat your customers nicely (*duh!*), but treat your employees nicer. By the way, we did solve the on-time delivery problem, and neither working harder nor working faster was the solution.

A careful audit from start to finish of the processes then in place throughout our product cycles revealed choke points that limited production rate to what was already being achieved. In other words, we were at maximum capacity, and no amount of administrative pressure or employee anxiety was going to change this for the better. The punishing effect of a business initiative destined to fail from the get-go for want of a strategy brought us to a state of economic stagnation. Focusing on these choke points and incorporating more efficient machining programs and workflow processes did the trick, enabling substantial growth within a short span of time. We worked smarter, not harder or faster. Consider the objectives you set for your business carefully and work cooperatively with your team to develop the strategies for achieving them. This is, in fact, the very definition of teamwork.

Despite our best efforts to avoid such situations, we sometimes found ourselves dealing with parties that intentionally or inadvertently caused disruptions that threatened the well-being of our company. These include cases in which major corporations simply stole our intellectual property despite agreeing to contracts strictly forbidding them to do so, causing us considerable financial hardship. These are the situations where sensibility serves you well. Sensibility means being aware, or *sensible*, to the people who supply your goods, compete in your market space, buy your products, and, yes, sometimes steal your trade secrets. I say *people* rather than businesses because, just like in your company, big or small, there are people making the decisions, writing the policies, and soiling the restrooms just like the rest of us. In every case, the source of attrition could be a personal character flaw, where some individual was making poor decisions based on an ill-conceived sense of self-preservation. You see, I think it is useful information for others in business to know how we navigated, successfully, through these obstacles and came out intact and perhaps even wiser for the experience. You will inevitably meet a variety of characters over the course of your career, no matter what professional space you exist in. Hell, I'm one of them, with quirks up to my ears, but if you plan on entering relationships with these people, acquaint yourself with them well because this is where the dealing is done, where the buck starts and stops. Fundamentally, all transactions, big and small, are between people. Make sure you know them by name and by character. This could be the most important lesson you take away from this book and apply to your business strategy. That, and taking great care to surround yourself with a solid, trustworthy team.

* * *

LIFE LESSON: *"Houston, we have a problem..."* Has there ever been a more resourceful, competent crack team than the Space Command Center engaged in a manned spaceflight mission? I mean, you can be soaring at meteor speed between the moon and Earth in a tin can with no means of steering, and they can get you home safely by duct taping some odds and ends together. But as capable as the Command Center team may be, there was little assistance they could provide to the spectacular Gemini Solar Orbit Mission, which turned out to be a one-way flight. One Christmas, Mike and I each received a limited-edition GI Joe set. Everything was limited edition back then. What made these special was that each Joe sported a fuzzy mustache and beard to emphasize his toughness. Mike had the Gemini astronaut edition, complete with Gemini space capsule and silver space suit, while I had the frogman edition, with a red scuba suit that matched his underwater sled. Mike was envious of the sled because it had an actual spinning propeller that would propel it across the bathtub, while the Gemini capsule just sort of sat there doing nothing. To get Mike more excited about his Gemini Joe, I suggested we play a game in which I would carry Joe and his capsule while Mike, taking on the role of

Command Center, would direct the mission. Mike followed me here and there with the two of us communicating in radio voices with simulated static, me addressing him as Command Center and he addressing me as Captain Joe. Eventually Captain Joe's mission led him out of doors, opening up new possibilities for exploration. My mother was burning brush in a steel fifty-five-gallon drum, and the capsule headed in its direction to investigate. Growing up, there was always some fire going on, often lit by the adults, so we could hardly be faulted for our fascination with it. Command Center raised concern of this being a hazard, but Captain Joe replied that he was wearing a silver fireproof suit that was meant for this very purpose. Imagine Captain Joe's dismay to learn that this blazing fire turned out to be the sun, and he was stuck in its gravitational pull. Command Center didn't like it much either. But as everyone knows, especially children, any object, even flammable ones, will pass through a flame unscathed if moving fast enough, and Gemini Joe could travel the speed of light. This proved true up until the third and final orbit when dizziness from spinning affected my balance and judgment, causing the capsule to contact the barrel rim and initiating an unscheduled re-entry. Joe and the capsule tumbled into the flames. Quick reaction on my part saved Joe but not the capsule, which could not be rescued before taking on a form undeniably unflight-worthy. Somehow Mike saw this as my fault and believed I owed him my water sled. I pointed out that his Joe was wearing a fireproof suit, so it was obvious he was designed for such adventures. A closer examination of the rescued Joe revealed his fuzzy hair and beard were gone, so I gave Mike the damned sled so as not to involve my mother in the negotiations. It was later discovered that Mike's GI Joe also had a deformed hand and could not be latched onto the water sled to operate it, so I had to relinquish my frogman Joe, too. That summer Joe was run over by the lawn mower. So it goes.

MORAL: Teamwork is a plan set into action while the mission is the fabric from which the team is sewn.

***

I'D LIKE TO SAY A final word on culture, which has been repeatedly emphasized throughout as a profound force impacting the shape and direction of a company. The formation of a culture within any business is inevitable and so must be deliberate. Attention must be paid during the early stages of your team building to ensure you are cultivating one that is robust and inspires the entire enterprise to thrive. If you find yourself endowed with a culture that does not serve the best interests of the company and its constituents, you can fix it. In fact, you must fix it, for a bad culture tends to get worse and is not likely to correct itself. I described how my company appointed an industry veteran boasting years of leadership experience at relatively large, well-structured corporations as our president. He oversaw all the managers and subsequently their departments and laid out a seemingly simple, comprehensive edict—*let's ship on time!* But it failed utterly and nearly led to a clandestine company-wide revolt. Our entire culture was somehow crushed, not right away but within the span of two years, and hardly anyone noticed. Or if they did, they kept quiet about it. Was it the edict? Unlikely. Was it the manner of execution? Probably. It's like the incident where Mike was stung over fifty times while I received nary a sting despite presenting an equal opportunity to the bees. Although we shared the same objective, i.e., *get the fuck out of there*, the stark difference in the methods of our escape influenced their behavior in favor of stinging Mike. It is the same with culture as with the beehive: if you behave in a way that is antagonistic or confusing to their interests, everyone gets pissed off, setting in motion a cascade of events nobody wants.

In our case, we worked with each individual employee (likely this would not have succeeded with the bees) to understand where the issues lay and how management could improve to satisfy their issues. The key was to partner with every affected employee one at a time. New employees and visitors to our facility all agree—we have a great culture, a family that genuinely enjoys working with one another. I am proud of how we turned our culture around and are reaping the benefits from it. If there is one thing I would like the world to know about our company, it is that we have a team of wonderful, exceptional people throughout the entire organization who love the business we have built together. That is the true meaning of success.

I leave you with these pieces of advice: (1) do not embark on your new business venture until you have completed a 4S assessment of yourself and have determined the person(s) needed to create a viable business, and (2) to succeed at anything, you first need to care.

Peace and love,
Charles McCarrick

Hank's Afterword

by Hank McCarrick

I FEEL NO NEED TO DEFEND MY ACTIONS FOR CONDITIONING my brothers for the real world, but I would like to explain the reason behind them. I was born an engineer. I didn't become an engineer due to some external influence; I was born an engineer. I am genetically compelled to take the visions stuck in my head and make them physical realities. Charlie derived a valuable lesson from the amusement park with the roller coaster ride, one of my most ambitious visions. While my knowledge of mechanics was acquired observationally at that age, my product testing and validation process was well ahead of its time. Things didn't always work as planned with my ideas, so this is where my younger brothers came in. They were my test engineers. I engaged them to ferret out imperfections in my creations through a well-thought-out failure analysis program. Lacking modern-day tools, my measurement for product performance was keeping a log of physical and emotional injuries. Fewer injuries to my brothers and less hiding in the woods from me were indications that we were zeroing in on perfection. As a result, I expected to be rich after we opened the amusement park to the public. That, however, did not go as planned, and I suffered my life's biggest regret. After we finished construction, I should have made Charlie CEO right then. I would now be half owner in Six Flags, and I could do all the rides for free.

> **LESSON LEARNED:** Always test your products thoroughly before taking them to market. One lawsuit from an injury and it's game over. Be thankful for the pioneers like my brothers who bravely sacrificed themselves so future product developers could sleep at night. Dick, I owe you big time for this well-learned lesson. And don't even think about suing me.

I want to clarify what really happened in some of the life episodes Charlie so colorfully describes. I trust my recollection of these as I was older and had a more developed mind. Charlie, on the other hand, was quite young and prone to seeing things in an exaggerated light. Let's start with the Olympic Stadium. As I recall, Charlie was my athlete of choice over my brother Dick. But the suggestion that I whipped them with a holly branch injures me deeply. It belittles the engineering skills I had acquired up to that point in time. A holly branch would not have served to inflict the necessary motivational pain I was seeking. I used a whip fashioned from a briar branch. Holly thorns are short, and the air friction imposed by holly leaves slows the velocity of the whip. A holly-branch whip would have served better as a comical prop to make my brothers laugh than as a motivational tool.

> **LESSON LEARNED:** When inspiring those you lead, always choose the most impactful tools for the job. Don't pussyfoot around. As that famous intellectual Arnold Schwarzenegger once said, "No pain, no gain."

Another example of Charlie's memory fog is giving my brother Bill credit for the handshake shock. I taught Bill this wonderful trick. To his credit, Bill did take this learned knowledge to extremes that surpassed even my imagination. The ability to produce this shock originated from our dad, who wired the cabin we lived in. Somehow, he missed properly grounding the electrical outlets. I discovered this in a way that almost killed me. The kitchen stove had left and right electric hotplates about two feet apart. If you stirred a pot on one hotplate, no problem. If you had two pots, each on its own hotplate, and stirred one with the left hand and the other with the right, 120 volts passed through your body by way of your heart. When I discovered this, I had a brief visit with God. God said a few words I didn't catch as my attention was focused on stepping back from the light. I quickly recovered and, not to lose the moment, immediately identified creative ways to share this experience with my family, which I was very eager to do. I showed this to my brother Bill first, and what a great learner he was. I was quite happy and proud when he passed this knowledge to Charlie.

LESSON LEARNED: All visionaries have had a near-death experience. This experience drives them to become the CEOs of their own companies. They soon discover they are ill-equipped for the challenge. To save the company, they find a competent CEO and become the chief strategy officer. The common explanation for stepping down is, "God told me to let go."

My electrifying experience in our ungrounded home did inspire me to develop a rule of thumb for business meetings. I would like to pass along this critical intelligence.

It's not good to be the only grounded person in a meeting. The workload that results will pass entirely through you. To avoid this, lift your feet off the floor and don't stir the pot.

I am thankful to my brothers for the data points they provided me along my engineering journey. Somehow, they seemed to have learned something from me as well. Though we weren't aware of it, we were all learning lessons that could enlighten others as soon as we were older, wiser, and 27.4 percent less mean. But this was not an all-boy theater. My older sister, Mary Ann (sorry, Sis, for the chronological placement), witnessed most of these adventures. Mary Ann had the early wisdom to distance herself from what had to appear as "brothers gone crazy." Perhaps the reason Mary Ann and I became great buds later in life is that she was spared being one of my test engineers.

Charlie's writings are a walk down memory lane and remind me of how much I love my family. Perhaps this translates to the most important lesson learned: *love those you work with as if they were your family.* I just wish some people wouldn't make that so damn hard, but I guess that is family, isn't it?

Charlie, I have learned much from you over the years. Thanks for being my teacher and educating me with a more tolerant and softer touch. I have always wondered if after we leave this planet there are revisits to our past lives. If so, while I can't promise, I will try to remember to trim down the briar thorns before implementing my motivational strategies as I chase you and Dick around Olympic Stadium.

—YLB, Hank

Jim's Afterword

by Jim Francis

IF YOU HAVE READ THIS FAR, YOU KNOW THAT CHARLIE IS indeed a funny man, and if you read to the end, you will know that, as he asserts, he is funnier than I. Charlie entitles this book *Lessons My Brothers Taught Me*, but a better title might be *Lessons in Life*. Charlie and I met at my house in Massachusetts, and he described a business deep with intellectual property (all inside of the man who became my dear friend) but in need of a plan to monetize the technology. In the process, we both were healed of terminal cancers and learned how to live with freedom. We did not quit. Charlie writes this book to entertain but more to teach principles of life.

I, too, have an older brother who specialized in tormenting me, teaching me business lessons as Charlie's brothers taught him.

* * *

LIFE LESSON: Bob and I shared a room with bunk beds. I was younger and slept in the lower bunk so that if I rolled out of the bed I would not be hurt. At age three I began asking Mom and Dad to let me sleep in the upper bunk. Bob would protest, saying that I couldn't because I would fall and be hurt. I was persistent, and one night my parents approved—with Bob declaring that I would fall out of the top bunk and hurt myself. I went to the top bunk, having achieved the reward for my persistence, and immediately fell asleep. The lights were turned off, and the door was closed. From the lower bunk, Bob put his feet under my mattress and thrust me into the air. I awakened in mid-air, screaming, and hit the floor. Parents arrived, and Bob announced, "I told you he would fall out." Bob was then given the upper bunk. Undaunted, I persisted the next day and the next.

MORAL: When your persistence results in success, expect adversaries to provide you the flight of your life. When you hit the ground, get up and continue to persist. Never quit.

* * *

WHEN WE BEGAN MAKING ANTENNA products that did not exist elsewhere in the world, our customers feared that once they began buying them and integrating them into their terminals, we would raise the prices, sell to competitors (creating a commodity), or stop making the antennas altogether. We gave them the following assurances:

- We will never raise prices.

- We will never create a competitor with the same product.

- We will never fail to deliver.

- We will persist and never quit.

These principles are fundamental to our company.

Soon we began to make a significant profit, and Charlie asked me, "What is our exit strategy?" Without thinking I replied, "A pine box?" I meant this literally. We will not exit Micro-Ant in the sense of selling the company to people who will dismantle it, or, as Charlie says, choke it to death. What we will do is continue to have the company grow and prosper with additional personnel and, at some point, additional owners who will, with us, maintain the culture and principles fundamental to the company.

ACKNOWLEDGMENTS

PLANET EARTH, AND BEYOND...

CPSIA information can be obtained
at www.ICGtesting.com
Printed in the USA
BVHW070927121122
651758BV00007B/379